Self-esteem

Other titles in this series:

Self-esteem

Theresa Francis-Cheung

Newleaf

Newleaf
an imprint of
Gill & Macmillan Ltd
Hume Avenue
Park West
Dublin 12
with associated companies throughout the world
www.gillmacmillan.ie

© Theresa Francis-Cheung 2002
0 7171 3333 8
Design by Vermillion Design
Illustration by Emma Eustace
Print origination by Linda Kelly
Printed by ColourBooks Ltd, Dublin

This book is typeset in Rotis Semi-Sans 10pt on 13pt.

The paper used in this book comes from the wood pulp of managed forests. For every tree felled, at least one tree is planted, thereby renewing natural resources.

A CIP catalogue record for this book is available from the British Library.

5 4 3 2 1

CONTENTS

INTRODUCTION

You are reading this book because you want to improve your self-esteem or help someone you care about build their self-esteem.

You've had a glance at the vast array of self-esteem books on the shelves and been daunted. You haven't got time to wade through pages and pages of technical jargon, therapeutic approaches, discussions, debates and diagrams which look like brain scans. You don't want to find your inner child, swim with the dolphins, visualise your funeral, detox until you are the living embodiment of purity, meditate, or take up yoga and tai chi. And you really aren't interested in endless case histories (which don't apply to your situation), personal anecdotes from the author (which always sound slightly implausible), wise proverbs (which never quite make sense), and all those 'ask yourself' lists and workshop-style exercises (does anybody really do those anyway?). You just want a book that will help you feel better about yourself, fast.

This is the book you are looking for! In no time at all this little guide will help you understand and improve the way you feel and think about yourself. You won't be bombarded with case studies, quizzes, exercises, proverbs, diagrams and my autobiography. You'll just get essential information and advice. Anything is possible when self-esteem is high, just as everything seems impossible when self-esteem is low. Let's not waste any more time and give you the knowledge and the skills you need to change your life for the better, right now.

CHAPTER 1

SELF-ESTEEM

Self-esteem is the way you think and feel about yourself. If you want to feel fulfilled, or to be comfortable in the company of others, self-esteem is crucial.

When you have self-esteem, 'life is just a bowl of cherries'.

You believe you are an OK human being. You are comfortable with yourself. You feel attractive and vital. You have confidence, energy and optimism. You trust the world and the people around you. You generally have positive or realistic expectations. You take positive action to meet your needs and wants. You accept responsibility for your failures and your successes and are willing to take calculated risks. You feel equal to other people. You feel a sense of pride, satisfaction and happiness with your life. You see problems as challenges and opportunities to learn and improve. When you wake up in the morning it's another day in paradise.

When self-esteem is low, 'life is doubt'.

You doubt yourself and those around you. You lack confidence. Instead of taking action, you worry. You are uncertain about what your needs and wants are. You see problems as obstacles. You blame yourself for your failures and don't take credit for your successes. You don't believe there is anything you can do to change. You rarely feel happy. When you wake up in the morning it's just another day you have to get through.

It doesn't take a psychology degree to work out from these two lists which person stands a greater chance of happiness in life. When self-esteem is low, your chances of happiness are low.

If you have low-self esteem you aren't being yourself, because you fear what others might think. You rely on others for approval. You don't think you are worthwhile and you have little faith in your own abilities. If anything good happens to you it is just luck, while the success of others is due to ability. You may relate to others by being servile, submissive, passive or overbearing and a little needy. You feel guilty when you say no. You probably say, 'sorry', 'yes, of course', and 'it's only me' quite a lot.

Sometimes self-doubt manifests in other ways. You may rely excessively on certain things for a feeling of self-worth. For instance, whether or not you feel good depends on your weight, your job, your finances, your home, your friends, or whether or not the man or woman of your dreams calls.

Or self-esteem may be high in one area of your life and low in others. You may feel confident at work and insecure in your relationships or vice versa. The trouble with this is that sooner or later lack of confidence in one area of your life is going to negatively affect other areas of your life. You need to feel relaxed and happy in all aspects of your life to function optimally.

And finally, your self-esteem could be good until something comes along, like losing a job or a relationship ending, to make you doubt yourself. Or pressures mount up in your life, and all of a sudden you feel doubtful, confused and frightened. At times even the most confident and happy among us feels insecure.

Whatever the cause, when self-esteem is low, the world you live in is a frightening and unpredictable one because you are always dependent on the whims of others or the turn of events. If you can compare your life to a car, when self-esteem is low you are not in the driving seat. Other people or events are steering the wheel, while you crouch in the back wondering where they will take you next. That's exactly what low self-esteem does to your life. You are alive, but you aren't really living.

WHAT SELF-ESTEEM ISN'T ABOUT

Our culture sets much store by self-esteem, as the shelves of self-help books on the subject prove. All too often we base our self-esteem on external factors such as looking good, having a partner, climbing the career ladder, gaining qualifications or having material possessions and wealth. All this is so fragile. Human beings age, lose jobs, fail in relationships, make mistakes and so on. The problem with self-esteem based on temporary externals is that you only feel good about yourself when things are going well, but when things don't go so well, you lose your self-esteem.

To prevent this, self-esteem needs to be grounded firmly in *self-acceptance*. The concept of self-acceptance is based on the knowledge that we are all fallible human beings, we all make mistakes and nobody is perfect. So although you would like to be 100 per cent perfect all the time, the important thing is to learn to accept that sometimes you will be wrong and you are fallible.

Self-esteem without self-acceptance sets you up for disappointments, stress and unhappiness when misfortune arises and self-esteem is attacked. You need to learn to accept yourself, warts and all. One advantage of this is that it becomes easier to accept others and their fallibilities.

WHAT ABOUT THE MEEK INHERITING THE EARTH AND ALL THAT?

Many of us misunderstand religious doctrines about forgiveness, obedience and humility. They don't mean becoming a doormat without opinions of your own or sacrificing your needs for those of others. They mean having the humility to recognise your weaknesses, respecting the opinions of others and working for the good of all concerned, including yourself.

High self-esteem isn't the same as selfishly serving your own interests and having an inflated idea of your own self-worth. You can easily spot the difference between a person with a healthy sense of self-esteem and a person who is arrogant. The former looks relaxed and is keen to listen and learn. Such people tend to make others feel better about themselves. The latter is keen to boast, rarely listens and likes the sound of his or her own voice. Such people tend to make others feel worse about themselves.

Improving your self-esteem isn't about becoming selfish, loud, competitive and arrogant. It's about taking care of yourself so that you have the strength and energy to help and give to others when appropriate. It's about being open-minded, assertive and confident in your abilities.

It's about being yourself, and knowing that within you lies the power to create all that you want in life.

CHAPTER 2

DO YOU HAVE IT?

You probably know already if you feel good or bad about yourself, but in case there is any uncertainty, the quiz below will help you. It's the only one in the book, so make the most of it.

On a scale of 1 to 10 how do you feel about yourself?

1 = extremely dissatisfied
2 = very dissatisfied
3 = moderately dissatisfied
4 = somewhat dissatisfied
5 = there are some things you like about yourself, but some things you don't
6 = okay
7 = somewhat satisfied
8 = moderately satisfied
9 = very satisfied
10 = brilliant

If your answer was under 6, your self-esteem is fragile to dangerously low. This book may be all that you need to get you back on track, but if you feel persistently hopeless and anxious (answer either 2 or 1) you might benefit from seeking advice from a doctor or other professional, such as a counsellor, minister or therapist.

If your answer was between 7 and 9, you don't really need this book, unless you are reading it to help someone else. If you answered 10, you are an inspiration to us all. Just be careful, though, that you don't become a 'big head'. Inflated self-esteem can be just as damaging as low self-esteem.

CHAPTER 3

WHY HAVEN'T YOU GOT IT?

Before moving on to self-help advice, let's pause first and think about why you have problems with self-esteem. Self-awareness is the starting point for all confidence-building programmes. The big question is why some people feel good about themselves and see life as an exciting challenge and why others feel bad about themselves and see life as a frustrating struggle.

WHAT CAUSES LOW SELF-ESTEEM?

For centuries, psychologists, doctors, health experts, scientists, religious leaders, politicians and self-help gurus have tried to answer this question. But at the end of the day the answer is always the same: no-one is really quite sure. Several factors may contribute. (Key words and terms are in italics.)

It's fashionable nowadays to blame mum and dad or your caregiver for everything. If *bonding*, the formation of a close personal relationship with parents, didn't occur, or you didn't form any kind of *attachment*, or emotional bond, with your caregivers, low self-esteem is likely. Bonding and attachment enhance self-worth because you experience feelings of being valued, which is an important factor in the development of a healthy self-esteem.

Approval, also known as *acceptance* and *affirmation*, is another crucial element in the development of your self-esteem. If you were accepted for who and what you are, without any preconceived ideas of what you should be or ought to do, of course you feel more secure than those who were constantly rejected, made to feel that they didn't match up to expectations unless they behaved in a certain way, or, most destructive of all, abused physically or verbally.

Rejection may not come from within the home. Low self-esteem could start with harsh criticism, rejection, ridicule or abuse outside the home, most commonly in school. The disapproving comments of teachers or negative nicknames like 'spotty', 'fatty' or 'four-eyes' are common examples of rejection. They can have an injurious and lasting impact on our sense of self-worth.

Everyone wants to be popular and accepted. Rejection hurts whatever age you are. It is hard to feel good about yourself when you get a negative appraisal at work, fail an exam or your partner tells you that he or she doesn't care about you anymore. All these things can injure self-esteem.

Genetics may hold a key to low self-esteem. People with low self-esteem often have parents or relatives who have problems asserting themselves. There is debate about whether this is *inherited* or *learned*. Children are born copycats. If you grew up seeing your parents always anxious and doubtful, you may not realise there are other ways to interact with the world.

Gender may also have a part to play. It is generally thought that women suffer from low self-esteem more than men, because of the conscious and unconscious indoctrination that men are somehow superior to women. Male superiority is, of course, a ridiculous notion, but traditional ideas of what it means to be a man and what it means to be a woman continue to linger on and do untold harm.

If men are indoctrinated to think that females are inferior, then so-called feminine qualities, like compassion, caring and sharing, may be repressed. And if women are brought up to believe that they are inferior, they may struggle with so-called masculine traits of strength, determination and intelligence. We all know men who can be caring and sharing and women who can be ruthless and ambitious. If these qualities aren't acknowledged for fear of what others might think, then these men and women are not being themselves. And it's when you aren't being yourself that self-esteem is low.

The foundations of low self-esteem are often laid in childhood, but as we grow up *stressful life events* and adult responsibilities can also cause self-esteem to plummet. Intimate relationships that don't work out, set-backs, knocks, poor health, accidents, the loss of a loved one, financial struggles and so on can all be damaging.

Depression and other *mood disorders* damage self-esteem, as can *addiction* to drink or drugs, *eating disorders*, and *compulsions*, such as a compulsion to exercise, have sex, gamble or clean. Depression is an illness that can be treated, but there is still great debate about whether or not mood disorders cause low self-esteem or low self-esteem causes mood disorders. If self-esteem is low, depression is more likely, but sometimes depression strikes for no apparent reason. If you are suffering from depression or any kind of compulsive behaviour, the advice in this book will help, but it is important that you also seek professional help.

As you reflect on your past, never lose sight of your goal, which is to change your life for the better. Self-esteem will not improve if you can't free yourself from the past. If you keep going back to the time your mum forgot to collect you from school or the fact that you were always the last choice for your form's sports team, it is time to take a deep breath and deal with the present. The past, however traumatic, can help you understand why you may feel a certain way but it can't explain why you choose to remain that way. Countless people have survived the most terrible ordeals and faced the greatest adversity with courage, optimism and a positive sense of who they are.

It's easy to look back and blame the past, your parents, your siblings, your teachers, your partner for leaving you, and so on, but at the end of the day the way you feel about yourself now is your responsibility. You can *choose* now to respond to life without your old self-doubt, hesitation and confusion.

Even if you feel that you were born a self-doubter, you can change. You can't change other people, but you can change yourself. I'll repeat that. *You can change.* Once you choose to improve your self-image you will feel happier and more fulfilled. If you want to change your life for the better, improving self-esteem is the first and only place to start.

CHAPTER 4

HOW CAN YOU GET IT?

So what will it take for you to feel good about yourself and lead the kind of life you want to live? How can you improve your self-esteem? It goes without saying that the most important thing is the *willingness to help yourself*.

If you are quite happy to complain endlessly about your life, to wait passively for someone or something to make things work for you, then this book won't help you. There may be hidden advantages to believing you are a defective or inferior person. For instance, you don't have the responsibility of making decisions, taking risks, or being accountable. If, on the other hand, you are willing to do something to solve your problems and improve your self-worth, the following strategies will help you.

This book is a Lazy Guide. I'm going to take lazy in the positive sense – you want to learn the basics quickly, not that you can't be bothered to make any effort. If you want to improve your self-esteem you will be required to make an effort, but as self-esteem improves you will soon discover that life gets easier.

You may not believe it, but staying the way you are takes far more effort. It's hard work worrying and feeling anxious all the time. It's hard work adjusting yourself constantly to the demands of other people and events. Life gets easier when you start taking care of yourself and start doing the things you want to do. It's a lot more fun, too!

SO, WHAT ARE THE SECRETS OF SELF-ESTEEM?

I have pinpointed eight strategies, or secrets, that can lead to lasting improvements in self-esteem. Here they are:

1. Get to know yourself.
2. Don't believe it because you think it.
3. Manage your emotions.
4. Improve your communication skills.
5. Make decisions.
6. Take care of yourself.
7. Manage stress.
8. Enjoy yourself.

In the chapters that follow we'll explore these strategies in more detail. They are fundamental to all self-esteem-building programmes, and it is important that you familiarise yourself with them. At the end of the day they hold the keys to improved self-esteem, happiness and a better life.

CHAPTER 5

GET TO KNOW YOURSELF

The first secret is about getting to know yourself better. It's time to start thinking about your life. How did your upbringing affect you? What is important to you? Are you doing what you want to do with your life?

Don't worry if you don't know the answers to any of these questions. The important thing is that you start asking them. In the chapters that follow you will be asked time and time again to reflect on why you think and feel the way you do. There is a reason for this. Each time you pause a little to think about who you are, why you do the things you do and why you feel the way you do, you will be getting to know yourself a little better.

Self-knowledge is the beginning of wisdom. Don't go overboard, though. As fascinating and remarkable as you are, keep interested in those around you and in other things. Your intention is to become more aware of who you are and why you do the things that you do, not to become narcissistic or obsessive. I've kept this chapter short for this reason.

It might help if you act as an observer on your own life. 'Step outside' yourself, and take a look at what you think, feel, say and do. This may sound a little crazy, but just have a go. It's a well-known technique to improve self-awareness. Watching yourself can really help you separate what you think and feel from who you are. You will see that throughout your day thoughts and feelings constantly flow through you. You will see that as powerful as these feelings and thoughts are, they are separate from you. You are the one who allows yourself to experience them. You are the one in charge.

You may be confident in some areas of your life but not in others. The key now is identifying those areas of your life that you want to change. Not being confident in one area of your life can negatively affect all areas of your life. How do you feel about the way you look, the work that you do, the relationships that you have, the food you eat, the clothes you wear? What things drag you down? What things lift you up?

If you want to build your self-esteem, then you need to start with secret number 1: self-awareness. That means looking at the way you live your life, the way you think and the way you feel. As you get to know yourself better you will start to recognise patterns of behaviour, responses or attitudes that make you unhappy.

And once you start to recognise what makes you unhappy you can start making positive changes. And the first of those changes needs to be in the way you think.

CHAPTER 6

DON'T BELIEVE IT BECAUSE YOU THINK IT

The way you think affects the way you feel. If you think you aren't worthwhile, then you won't feel worthwhile. Becoming aware of how your thoughts are affecting the way you feel about yourself is a big step forward.

> Try this simple exercise. Think of something really sad, like a funeral. Now think of a time when you felt really happy, like a holiday. You will notice immediately how your thoughts affect your feelings.

If you constantly think of yourself in a negative light, thoughts like 'I'm useless' or 'I can't cope' start to become ingrained. Think negatively for long enough, and you may not even be aware that you are doing it anymore.

Sometimes it might seem that you aren't in charge of your thoughts. This isn't true. The second secret to self-esteem is understanding that you are in charge of what you think about. Once you start to recognise how negative thought patterns affect the way you feel about yourself, you can start to replace them with other thoughts.

You don't have to replace negative thoughts with positive ones, simply with more appropriate ones. Positive thinking can be as unhelpful and as unrealistic as negative thinking. Always looking on the bright side when things are clearly falling apart around you won't do you any good at all.

Negative thoughts need to replaced with more realistic ones, but fortunately realistic thoughts are much more optimistic than negative ones. Realistic thoughts take into account the negative, but they also take into account other possibilities. For example, saying to yourself, 'I'm no good at anything' can be replaced by 'There are things I'm not good at, but there are also things I'm good at.'

When negative thoughts start to appear, evaluate them carefully. Don't treat them automatically as facts because you are thinking them. The trick is to recognise when you have a negative thought and to ask yourself, 'Am I being realistic?' If you aren't being realistic you need to replace it with something more constructive.

From now on, every time you have negative thoughts about yourself – typical ones are listed below – start challenging them with reason, realism and facts.

EXAGGERATING

Self-doubters often make mountains out of molehills. A small set-back becomes a major disaster. 'I totally messed that up' may refer to a small mistake; a minor cold is a near-death experience.

Exaggerating only makes you feel even more out of your depth. Try to get into the habit of describing situations as they are and not dramatising them. This will help you feel more in control. Okay you made a mistake.

I'VE FAILED AGAIN

Everyone makes mistakes. In fact, the most interesting,

exceptional people are the ones who make the most. The only way to learn about your strengths and your weaknesses is to make mistakes. Making mistakes builds character.

Negative thinking can really handicap you when you are trying to achieve a new goal or solve a problem. Every mistake you make will be interpreted as a failure and proof of your inadequacy. Of course failures can be devastating, but they can also help you grow and learn about yourself and what you do and do not want in life. You can gain something from every experience, however disappointing. Seen in that light, there is no such thing as a failure.

Remember it's not what happens to you but how you *react* to what happens to you that determines your self-worth. If you failed an exam, find out what your weakness was and try again. If you didn't get the job you wanted, find out why and use that knowledge to improve your chances at the next job you apply for.

Rather than labelling your mistakes or disappointments as failures, try to view them as set-backs or learning experiences. This is less final than failure. Think in terms of temporary set-backs, which add to your store of knowledge whenever you feel disappointed or let down. That way you will feel less inclined to give up and more willing to try again.

THAT'S IT, I CAN'T DO IT

Negative thinkers often tend to think that if something has gone wrong once it will always go wrong.

You have a bad day at work and you decide that you aren't good at your job.

You have an argument with your partner and decide the relationship is in crisis.

Everywhere you turn there are examples of set-backs leading to success. Walt Disney, Steven Spielberg and J. K. Rowling are just a few examples of people whose ideas were initially rejected but who eventually achieved spectacular success. Sometimes when you are tuning in to a radio station you get the wrong wavelength. You keep fiddling with the tuner until you get the quality of reception that you want. Persistent effort pays off. Just because you didn't get the station the first time doesn't mean that you will never get it.

If you are prone to generalisation and sweeping conclusions whenever you have a set-back, you need to start challenging your thought patterns.

I had a bad day at work but I am still good at what I do.

We had an argument, but it does not mean we need to head for the divorce courts. We are still doing fundamentally fine.

Don't let yesterday's or today's disappointments stop you from succeeding tomorrow. Nobody knows what the future holds. You may have had a set-back yesterday, but it's entirely possible things will work out tomorrow. Something minor may have gone wrong, but a disaster is not soon to follow. If you were disappointed today, tell yourself, 'It didn't happen today, but tomorrow is another day.'

IT'S MY FAULT

Humankind is always trying to explain why things happen. If things don't work out, we want to find someone to blame. We blame others. People with low self-esteem blame themselves.

Never accept blame for things that are out of your control. Don't concentrate solely on your weaknesses – turn your attention to your positive aspects and signs of your strengths. Fix your strengths firmly in your mind, and be ready to remember them, especially when things go wrong. If something unfortunate does happen, get out of the habit of saying it's your fault because you aren't good enough. You may make mistakes, but you are still a worthwhile human being. Try to replace blaming thoughts with encouraging ones: 'This didn't work out, but how was I to know this or that would happen?'

It is impossible for you to be in control of all the factors that create a situation.

FORTUNE TELLING!

Some things are likely to happen. The sun will rise in the morning and set in the evening. At night the moon and stars will come out. But there is no such thing as complete certainty. The world probably won't, but it could, end tomorrow!

When you start to see only the negative, you lose a sense of perspective. You also forget that you are only human. You can't see into the future. How do you know that things are going to go horribly wrong? If you are prone to negative thinking, it's likely that your predictions favour negative outcomes. Nobody can tell what the future holds. It is unlikely that everything will turn out unpleasant all the time. Your predictions are unrealistic and biased.

If you keep searching the future for things you fear, start challenging that thinking now. How do you know? If you think you know what other people are thinking, question that assumption. You can never know what someone else is thinking. You can only guess.

It's more realistic to think that unpleasant things may or may not happen. It's more appropriate to conclude that someone is likely to think this, but you are not a mind reader. Things may turn out bad, but they may also turn out right. Allow yourself the possibility that things may go right. Get rid of over-the-top pessimism.

IGNORING THE POSITIVE

This stage in the downward spiral of negative thinking is the bleakest of all. You don't think anything can go right anymore. You reach a point where you can't see any meaning. You are tempted to give up. But life is full of disappointment and futility only if you think it is.

If you don't think you will ever meet the partner of your dreams, remind yourself that love works in mysterious ways. You can find Mr or Mrs Right in the most unexpected ways. Challenge negative thoughts as much as you can by looking for facts to disprove them.

You will start to learn that negative thinking not only makes you feel unhappy, it is also misleading and inaccurate.

WORRY

Unless you find a way to manage worry, it tends to get worse and worse. Negative possibilities get magnified out of all proportion. For instance, one mistake at work and before you know it you are questioning your ability to do your job. Disturbing thoughts do seem to fly into our minds a lot, but you don't need to nurture them. Remember that you are in control of your thoughts. You may not be able to stop worry happening, but you can learn to cope with worry in a positive way.

The next time you start worrying, try the following:

- Stop and recognise that you are worrying.

- Try to identify what is worrying you. If you don't know and just feel negative and anxious, see worry as a helpful warning sign that something in your life isn't working.

- Ask yourself, 'Is there anything I can do to change the situation?' If there is, get on and do it. If there isn't, change your attitude to the situation and find a substitute for the energy your worry is using up.

- If worry makes you tense, learn to relax your muscles.

- If worry is preventing you from making a decision think of all the possible alternatives, weigh up the pros and cons and take action. If mistakes occur, remind yourself that nobody can be 100 per cent right all the time. Learn from the set-back and try again.

- Most of the time worry is influenced by irrational thinking processes. Past events may be influencing the way you react to current situations, or faulty beliefs may cause problems. For instance, if you were rejected by your parents you may feel that unless you win the approval of others you are worthless. Or you may feel that unless you act a certain way people won't like you.

It's time to start asking yourself questions again. Do you have any faulty or irrational beliefs that need to be replaced with more positive ones?

FINDING AN ALTERNATIVE WAY TO THINK

When you start becoming more familiar with your thinking biases, you can challenge them in the ways suggested above.

Secret number 2 sounds so simple, but in practice you may find it harder than you think. The key is practice. You are learning a new skill. You are learning to talk to yourself in a reassuring and supportive way. Your negative thoughts aren't used to being challenged. Keep practising, and in time challenging them will become second nature. You will start recognising when you are losing perspective, worrying too much and seeing only the negative.

One day, constant put-downs and negative assessments of your ability won't seem so compelling anymore. They may even start to seem melodramatic, unrealistic and slightly absurd.

CHAPTER 7

MANAGE YOUR EMOTIONS

In the last chapter we looked at challenging negative thinking. In this chapter we'll progress to the third secret to better self-esteem: managing your feelings.

Emotional confidence is particularly important for building self-esteem. It is the ability to be fully in charge of your feelings and to express the full range of emotions without worrying that you will lose control. It is expressing your feelings appropriately and responding sensitively to the feelings of others.

If you are emotionally confident, you don't say things such as:
'I don't know what I feel.'
'I don't know what came over me.'
'I couldn't stop myself.'
'I don't know what's happened to me.'

Having feelings that 'make' you act in ways that run counter to your values is damaging to self-esteem. If your feelings are not 'making' you act in ways you don't want to act, self-esteem will improve and you will have a firmer sense of your own identity. You will be more consistent in the ways you react and behave. Because you are aware of the influence your feelings have on your reason, you will find it easier to make decisions and see the opportunities rather than the problems that come into your life.

If you find that your feelings start to get in the way of your doing what you want to do with your life, or being the kind of person you want to be, it is time to take positive action. Rock-solid emotional confidence is an impossible ideal, but there are things you can do to improve the way you handle your emotions.

You may find it hard to understand or trust your emotions. Sometimes they seem so illogical, and we have been conditioned to delay or deny their expression. Yet the very nature of our emotions is to be illogical. Sometimes, for instance, you just feel sad. Instead of questioning and denying, simply allow yourself to feel sad.

You may find it painful to express your emotions, but feelings, including the so-called negative ones such as anger, fear, sadness, will lead to improved self-esteem. This is not to say that we should act on them all the time, but you should acknowledge that these emotions exist in order to alert you to an area of discomfort in your life. When emotions are not felt, they cause even greater stress because you are not allowing yourself to feel what is true for you. Emotions are messages that come from your inner wisdom. If they are not worked through, the biochemical effect of suppressed emotions may cause physical and emotional tension.

Emotions are the only real way we have to show what matters to us and what doesn't. Difficult emotions signal the need for some kind of change in our lives. They require us to act, to change the situation or mind-set that is causing distress, to move on with our lives. Negative emotions are not bad emotions; they are necessary for us to grow and develop.

Reconnecting with your emotions won't be easy if you have been used to denying or suppressing them, but it is important that you do start to become more aware of what you are feeling. Once you start to become more aware of your feelings and have allowed yourself to feel them, it's time to try and deal with them. Understanding why you are feeling a certain way may help, but do remember that sometimes you won't know why you are feeling as you do. There may also be times when you feel confused and aren't sure what you are feeling.

WHEN YOU DON'T KNOW WHAT YOU ARE FEELING

When you are confused about your feelings, you may find yourself reacting inappropriately in certain situations. Here are a few suggestions to help you cope:

■ Recognise that emotional confusion can be caused by feelings from the past leaking into your present situation. For instance, if your first partner was unfaithful, you may become extremely jealous of your current partner even if he or she is giving you no cause.

■ Explore emotional pain from your past. Think about how your upbringing or past experiences may be affecting you.

■ Understand that you may not see clearly. If a feeling from an unhealed wound is echoed in the present – for example, if someone you trusted abused you – you may have problems trusting anyone again.

■ Recognise that you may not be able to heal every emotional wound, but you can choose how much it will control your life. Some hurts cut so deep they seem to scar us permanently. Yet it is possible to reach a stage where that hurt doesn't undermine our confidence anymore.

ACCEPT, CHOOSE AND MANAGE

Managing your emotions is a book in itself, so this section is by necessity brief. When you begin to notice that your emotions are hurting you or someone else, remind yourself that you are in charge of your feelings. Your feelings are not in control of you. Nothing can make you feel angry, sad, guilty or frightened unless you allow them or it to. Think about what your feelings are trying to tell you.

This simple strategy might help:

Accept

The first step in managing emotions is to accept what you are feeling, try to understand that feeling, and take responsibility for it, even if it is troublesome or embarrassing. For instance, if you feel sad don't deny that you are feeling sad or blame other people for making you feel that way.

Choice

The next step is to choose how you respond to that emotion. In many cases you may wish to use a strategy to induce a state of calm within yourself. That way, when you act, you are acting out of your whole self rather than just out of the emotion. For instance, sometimes when you feel sad it helps to have a good cry, or talk to a friend, or just spend time alone.

Manage

Finally, you need to manage the destructive habit that encourages your feelings to overwhelm and confuse you. Throughout the process, remind yourself that managing your feelings can only enrich your experience of life. Feeling something is far, far preferable to feeling nothing at all.

MANAGING SPECIFIC EMOTIONS

Before we move on, let's take a quick look at specific feelings that, when they are too intense, have the potential to damage your self-esteem. Instead of feeling bad about yourself when you feel these emotions, try these suggestions for taking positive action. You may be able to do this alone, or with the support of family and friends, or you may need the guidance of a therapist.

Sadness and disappointment

When you feel sad or disappointed, life seems to turn a shade of grey. It's hard to feel good about yourself. When sadness strikes, the following may help:

■ Determine the cause if you can.

■ Release some of the feelings. Basically, have a good cry!

■ Comfort yourself, and/or accept the support and comfort of others.

■ Get a sense of perspective, and try to salvage a positive aspect from the experience.

■ If you can, find a constructive way to use the experience of your hurt to benefit yourself or others.

■ If you can, forgive who or what was responsible for the hurt, even if it was you, and put the hurt firmly behind you.

■ If the feelings of sadness become too overwhelming, seek medical advice.

Guilt

Guilt is especially damaging to self-esteem. When guilt rules, life isn't about being who you are and doing what you want to do, it is about 'shoulds' and 'oughts'. When you feel guilty:

■ Think about what values you have inherited from your past and which are likely to trigger episodes of guilt.

■ Think about what your values are, not those of others.

■ Keep your assertiveness skills going so that you can defend those values. (We'll talk more about this later.)

■ Keep a sense of perspective.

■ Be realistic about your own skills.

■ Learn from your mistakes.

■ If you hurt someone, make amends if you can.

■ Get support from those who respect and value you for who you are, not what you do.

Shame

When you feel ashamed, self-esteem plummets. The following may help:

■ Acknowledge emotional wounds from the past.

■ Stop putting yourself down.

■ Focus on your strengths, not your weaknesses.

■ Be good to yourself.

■ Accept support from others who respect and value you and

accept you the way you are.

- Be yourself, and stop playing a role to be what others expect you to be.

- Think about what you want.

Anger

Sometimes it is important to feel anger, but when anger gets out of hand it can be damaging.

- Deal promptly with minor threats so that tension doesn't built up.

- Think about what is worth getting angry about and what isn't.

- Understand what triggers episodes of anger, and make a plan to counteract that.

- Boost your self-esteem so that you aren't vulnerable to attack.

- Practise stress management techniques. (We'll talk more about this later.)

- Find an activity that releases pent-up tension.

- Find a way to channel your anger, such as studying or starting a new hobby.

- Pay attention to your social support network.

- If you did lose your cool, reflect on what went wrong and how you could behave differently next time.

Fear

Fear is one of the most limiting emotions. It stops you doing what you want with your life. When fear threatens to become overwhelming:

■ Practise correct breathing and stress management techniques.

■ Talk to yourself in a constructive, positive way.

■ Work through fear in small, manageable steps.

■ Rehearse before going into stressful situations so that you are mentally prepared.

■ Imagine yourself being calm, and bring that image to your mind.

Jealousy

Wanting other people to behave in a certain way can poison relationships. If you catch yourself feeling jealous, the following might help:

■ Don't constantly analyse your relationships; try to enjoy being in them.

■ If you do get rejected, take time to heal, and don't blame yourself.

■ Keep your life outside your relationships full and satisfying to promote your self-esteem.

■ Keep making new friends.

■ Learn to value the importance of personal space and solitude.

Envy

Wanting things you cannot have can injure self-esteem. The next time you feel envious:

- Think about the times you have been lucky and the times when life has given you a break.

- Think of envy as a piece of information telling you what you really want for yourself. Add this to your personal goals.

- If your goals are achievable, see if they merit the attention you are giving them. Do you really want them so badly? If you do, replace envy with realistic, achievable goals for yourself.

- If your goals are unachievable, replace them with realistic ones.

- Always keep a sense of what you value and what your goals are.

Apathy

If self-esteem is so low that you don't want to make any effort anymore, you can do some things to get back on track:

- Keep mentally and physically active.

- Visit new places, meet new people and do new things.

- Don't accept everything you are told at face value.

- Try to eat healthily and get enough sleep.

- Learn new things.

- If you have reached the point when you don't feel anything at all anymore, you could be suffering from depression. Depression is a medical condition that improves with treatment. Seek medical advice immediately.

Loving too much

When self-esteem is low, love can become confused with need.

Relationships suffer and often don't survive. To avoid becoming too dependent on another person or group of people:

- Value the importance of personal space and solitude.

- Nurture yourself.

- Have more than one key relationship.

- Don't neglect everything else when you start a special relationship.

- Be on your guard if a person wants to change you.

- Be assertive in your relationships.

- Always remember what you want in a relationship.

- Don't put anyone on a pedestal.

Throughout the process of coming to terms with your emotions, always try to seek out the positive potential in every emotion and not just the negative. Remember nothing in life is ever wholly good or bad. Sometimes it's good to feel angry or sad or slightly envious. Managing your emotions will give you the confidence to be the person you want to be. That's why it's secret number 3 on the path to better self-esteem.

REVIEW TIME

So let's review what we've talked about so far. You are starting to become more self-aware, to question negative thoughts and to understand and manage your emotions. Hopefully you will begin to recognise that you make yourself unhappy when you dwell on unhappy things.

That's tremendous. You are well on the way to changing your life for the better. Before we move on, you might want to put your feet up for a while and reflect on all that you are learning. Do come back to the book though; there are some more things you need to know and do.

CHAPTER 8

IMPROVE YOUR COMMUNICATION SKILLS

If you can't communicate well with others, self-esteem is likely to remain fragile. You won't be able to get your point of view across or your needs met and this can make you feel more inadequate and useless.

Talking is a natural skill but effective communication – the fourth secret to better self-esteem – needs to be learned. The following suggestions may help.

- *Learn to listen.* Allow other people to express their thoughts and feelings without constantly interrupting with your own. If you try to understand and be attentive to the needs of others, you will find yourself better understood. Really listen to what others are saying. Don't think about what your response will be. Don't advise or criticise. Be reflective in your listening. Restate or reflect back what the other person has said to you to show that you have been listening.

- *Communication is a two-way process*, and as well as listening to someone else, you will also want them to listen to you. But wait until a person is ready to listen to you. If they are not ready to listen, they won't hear what you have to say. When they are receptive, ask if they understand what you are communicating.

- *Don't be afraid of silence in conversations.* In times of silence you can collect your thoughts. A great deal can be said in times of silence: 'I'm listening. I'm understanding. I'm there for you.'

■ *Effective communication takes place only with feedback.* Feedback gives both people a chance to avoid misunderstandings. You signal to the other person by the response that you make that you understand what they are saying. Communication often breaks down when one or both people don't understand each other.

■ *The aim is to make someone aware of what has been done and the feelings it arouses in you in such a way as to make the other person not feel that they are to blame.* You don't blame the person; you focus the attention on the consequences. For instance, 'When you said that it made me feel anxious' instead of 'You are making me feel anxious.'

■ Words carry many meanings and the art of communication is to understand fully what the other person is trying to convey. Avoid: questions that require a no or a yes answer, questions that are leading, questions that are interrogating.

■ Use questions that facilitate communication, for instance, 'What happened?' or 'How do you feel about that?'

■ And finally, *make sure that when you communicate you are as direct as possible.* Say what you mean, but without causing offence. In other words, be diplomatic. Don't tell someone that you don't like the coat they are wearing, tell them you don't think the coat flatters them.

Not being able to communicate effectively puts you at a disadvantage in establishing relationships and seriously affects self-esteem, because you don't make emotional contact with other people. If your self-esteem is low it's often hard to communicate effectively with others and you might benefit from assertiveness training.

ASSERTIVENESS

The goal of assertiveness is to confront without undermining yourself or others. The assertive person knows what they want, decides if what they want is fair to everyone concerned, and asks for it clearly and calmly.

It is easier to be assertive if you are relaxed, calm and well prepared. Stress, anxiety and worry will undermine your ability to be assertive. It helps to be encouraging and as positive as you can when you are trying to get your point across. Objectivity is important for keeping calm and focused. Keep your request brief, and don't get personal. Say how a person's behaviour or actions have affected you, not how that person him or herself has affected you. For example, 'I get upset whenever you do that', not 'You're upsetting me'. The emphasis now is on what that person did, not who that person is.

Your aim is not to win or make someone agree with you, but to find a solution that suits everyone. This will involve a certain amount of compromise and negotiation. Negotiation gets easier if you follow these suggestions:

Really listen to and understand what the other party is saying.
Avoid nerves by being prepared.
Keep calm.

Refrain from criticising the other party.

Keep to the point being discussed.

Be prepared to compromise, take risks, or back down if you have to.

To become more assertive, you need to learn to improve the way you communicate what you want or believe to others in a manner that is respectful of yourself and of others. This doesn't mean opting out of conflict and taking a passive approach or being loud, aggressive and overpowering, or being manipulative, devious and undermining; it means seeing all sides of the situation and recognising your needs and the needs of other people.

It sounds hard, but it really isn't. Keep practising and you'll get there. Start with little things, like making sure the food you order in a restaurant is prepared the way you like it. Don't blame the waiter or throw a tantrum, just calmly say what the problem is and ask for it to be corrected. If you can offer a sincere compliment, the waiter is more likely to want to help you. Nine times out of ten you'll get the dish the way you like it. If you don't, take your business elsewhere. In no time at all you'll be practising your assertiveness skills in more important areas of your life.

DEALING WITH CRITICISM

Criticism can come in many forms, but the basic intention behind them all is the same: to undermine you in some way. To deal with this you need to develop skills that help you stand your ground. One of these is not to take no for an answer. Repeat your message, however persistent or manipulative the other person gets, until that person has heard what you say and agreed to negotiate with you. Another way is to acknowledge that there may be an element of truth in the criticism, yet follow that up with an assertion of your viewpoint: 'I understand what you are saying, but I still feel ...' You may also decide to agree with the criticism, depending on the nature of it, or actively encourage it to find out whether your critic is being truthful or manipulative.

Criticism from others can destroy self-esteem. Criticism hurts. Much, of course, depends on the spirit in which the criticism was given. If it was intended to help you correct and improve, then see criticism as an opportunity to learn and grow, but if the criticism was unjust, how do you cope with that?

You may want to bear in mind that unjust or unfair criticism is usually given to make the critic feel important. It often means that you are worthy of attention and the critic feels jealous or threatened. So the next time you receive unjust criticism, try taking it as a compliment.

Gender-related criticism

Expectation placed on you because of your gender, or judgments made about you, can destroy confidence. Your gender may force you to confront roles you are not content with, or make you feel anxious about issues that concern the other sex less.

This is a generalisation, and there are many exceptions, but women often feel trapped in the role of caretaker. Low self-esteem is linked to issues surrounding sexual harassment, lower-paying jobs, limited career opportunities, unequal treatment and social expectations of how to look and behave. For men it is often linked to lack of intimacy, emotional repression, social expectation and the obligation to provide financial support.

Creative solutions can be found for gender-related issues. Most of them involve confronting and letting go of stereotypes you or others may have, being clear about who you are and what you want and setting reasonable goals for yourself. The same applies to anxiety about sex or sexual orientation, worries related to religious, cultural and ethnic background and worries related to physical appearance.

If any of the personal issues above make you feel uncomfortable about yourself, working on self-acceptance is your first step. Put simply, that means liking yourself and having confidence in yourself no matter who you are, what you look like, where you come from, where you are going and what others say about you.

If you don't think you are good enough, attractive enough, popular enough or talented enough, ask yourself: Am I being realistic? No-one is completely good or wholly bad. Stop focusing entirely on the negative and allow the positive into the picture.

IT'S OKAY TO SAY NO

In the last chapter we saw how it is okay to feel angry. It's what you do with that anger that is important, not the fact that you feel angry. The key is learning to channel anger in a positive way. It's the same with saying no.

If your self-esteem is low, you may be one of those people who can't say no. You are probably letting your kids or your partner or your friends get away with murder. You are probably embarrassed by praise or criticism and have trouble coping with people. It's likely that you have the best of intentions and are incredibly loving and giving, but the trouble is that everyone takes advantage of you and, unfortunately, at the end of the day no-one respects you.

If other people are walking all over you, it is time to start practising assertiveness skills. The only person who has the right to judge your behaviour, thoughts and emotions is you. You have the right to change your mind, say no or 'I don't understand', or 'I don't know', or even 'I don't care'.

If you are helping others because you really want to, that's fine, but if you are frightened of becoming unpopular or lonely if you stop being everything to everybody, remind yourself that those who really care about you won't put unwelcome demands on you. If you start feeling obligated or guilty in your relationships, then it is time to change the dynamic of those relationships and, if need be, move away from them.

As you work on secret number 4, and your communication skills start to improve and you get better at asking for what you want – and saying no if you need to – you are perfectly poised to take on the next challenge in your self-esteem-building programme: decision making.

CHAPTER 9

MAKE DECISIONS

If your self-esteem is low, you probably have a hard time making decisions. Worry and self-doubt make it virtually impossible to take any action at all. When action isn't taken and you don't make decisions, you get stuck in uncertainty and confusion.

Here are some things you can do to help you with secret number 5 on the path to better self-esteem: decision making.

- First, *find out what the problem is and whether or not you can do something about it.* Try to solve only the problems you have a chance of solving.

- *Be as specific about your problems as you can.* If you have lots of worries, the best thing to do is to tackle them one at a time. Putting certain worries on hold will be difficult, because the whole purpose of worry is to capture your attention, but you can't deal with everything at once. Solving one worry at a time will make you feel less stressed.

- Second, *list as many ways as you can of dealing with the problem.* Give yourself as much choice as possible. The more choice you have, the more chance you have of selecting a way of coping that is right for you. This is also called brainstorming. List as many solutions as you can even if they seem far-fetched. Suspend your judgment and all the reasons why this or that isn't a good solution, and let those ideas come.

■ When you've listed as many solutions as you can, even the trivial and outrageous ones, *now it's time to make a decision.*

DECIDING WHAT TO DO

When choosing between options, you need to ask yourself what you really want to happen. Remember, your real needs aren't always easy to recognise. You may want something, but you may also feel that others expect something of you. You may have taken on board ideas and values that don't really reflect who you are. It is important when you make a decision that it reflects what you want and not what others expect of you.

When you consider an option ask yourself if this is what you want to do, or if it is what your partner, your family or your friends want you to do. For instance, do you really want the job you are applying for? If you are always thinking in terms of should and ought, start thinking in terms of what you want or, better still, what is in everybody's best interests – including your own. Are you acting according to your own feelings or someone else's?

Once you become more attuned to your own feelings and what you want, life gets a lot easier. You start doing what you feel is right and not what others feel is right for you. You start considering choices you previously wouldn't consider.

DON'T SET UNREALISTIC GOALS

Earlier I suggested that when you think of solutions to a problem you list as many choices as you can, even ones that seem impossible or unrealistic. Doing so can help you dream up as many solutions as possible and stop you thinking that there isn't an answer. However, once you have thought of a number of coping strategies, it is time to use your common sense. Don't try to solve a problem in a way that isn't suited to your abilities. We all have limitations. Problems often test our limitations.

If you set unrealistic goals, you set yourself up for failure and unhappiness. Be careful. Don't try to solve a problem that requires skills you don't have or can't acquire.

If you keep approaching a problem in a way that has failed for you in the past, try to change your approach. Consider if the solution you are choosing fits the demands of the coping strategy you have selected. For instance, if you still can't lose weight after years of dieting, consider a new approach to eating, exercise and health.

PUTTING A SOLUTION INTO PRACTICE

In very specific ways, decide what will be done, how it will be done, when it will be done, where it will be done, who is involved and what your back up plan is if something goes wrong. For instance, you may decide that you do really want to change jobs and you are going to apply for a new one. You decide not to tell your employer unless you get the job. If possible, rehearse in role play or imagination your chosen solution. Now you are ready to move to the final stage: putting your solution into action.

Make sure you are well prepared and try your solution. Whether or not the solution is successful, review it and see what you can learn from the experience.

If your solution worked, congratulate yourself. You may, for example, be offered the job of your dreams. Perhaps you might like to treat yourself. If you aren't used to treating yourself, think about something you would like, and indulge yourself. The important thing is to acknowledge your successes. Also make time to think about why your solution worked and what you can learn about your strengths and weaknesses from it.

If your solution didn't work, don't torture yourself with worry and anxiety. Try to understand why it didn't work. Say you didn't get offered the job you wanted. Perhaps you just didn't have enough experience. Perhaps you didn't take something into account. Maybe you weren't feeling strong that day, or you misinterpreted something, or you didn't have a back up plan or were not prepared enough.

Whatever conclusion you reach, remind yourself that you have not failed. You've gained more information about what it will take to succeed the next time. Congratulate yourself for having had the courage to try. Learn as much as you can from the experience, and with the knowledge that you have gained, select another solution and try again. The more solutions you try, the more you will learn and the better equipped you will be to deal with the situation.

It isn't the end of the world if your coping strategy failed. You can always try another one or go back to the beginning and define the problem again. Don't be discouraged by set-backs. It's impossible to know what will happen in the future. Treat each attempt to solve a problem as if it is the first, however long it takes.

WHAT IF I MAKE THE WRONG DECISION?

No-one likes to make mistakes, but it is impossible to go through life without making them. In fact, the most successful people are often the ones who make the most mistakes. A large part of their success is that they view mistakes not as failures but as learning experiences. They understand that you can't always know what is right and sometimes you just have to take a risk. If things don't work out, they find out what went wrong, learn from the experience and try again.

Self-esteem is not about banishing frustration and disappointment, but about learning how to manage negative feelings and experiences. Mistakes, set-backs and disappointments are part of life and an important part of how we learn and grow. The main difference between those who succeed in life and those who don't is their attitude toward disappointment and difficulty. The person with healthy self-esteem isn't the person who never makes mistakes, but the person who learns from their mistakes and knows how to make the best of them.

WHAT IF YOU CAN'T MAKE A DECISION QUICKLY?

Of course, hasty decisions are a bad idea, but the problem-solving approach recommended above advises defining a problem carefully and considering all the pros and cons. This isn't being hasty. Unfortunately, though, when self-esteem is low you may find yourself paralysed by indecision. You may go over and over the same things again and again in an effort to be sure you are 100 per cent right.

Sometimes there isn't enough evidence to make it certain that a particular solution is the right one. If you are paralysed by indecision on a regular basis, it is time to start becoming accustomed to taking sensible risks. You can't tell for sure what will happen, but life experience and common sense will give you a pretty good idea. Start by making decisions about things that aren't too serious. For instance, there are two coats you like in a shop, but you only want one. Don't agonise for ages; just consider the pros and cons and make a decision. Even if in hindsight you make the wrong choice, this isn't the end of the world. Does it really matter? You could always give the first coat to a friend and buy the other coat another time.

After you have practised with smaller decisions, move on to harder ones. Each time a decision needs to be made, remind yourself:

■ Worry is a natural reaction to a possible problem.

■ Decision making isn't always followed by catastrophe.

■ The quicker you deal with the problem, the less time you will spend worrying.

■ You can't be 100 per cent certain of anything.

■ If you have thought about a problem, evaluated the pros and cons, and considered what is in everyone's best interests, including your own, you are not being hasty.

In the past, decision making may have been associated with anxiety, sleepless nights and poor concentration. It is time now for you to break these associations. When a decision needs to be made, think of any anxiety you may have as a helpful signal telling you that something isn't quite right. Try to associate decisions not with anxiety, but with positive change. Hopefully, in time secret number 5 – decision making – will become easier and the association with fear will break down.

WILL MAKING DECISIONS MAKE ME FEEL BETTER ABOUT MYSELF?

Without a doubt. Life is about doing, not thinking about doing. When you start facing your fears, you will find that you start to worry less about them. Your energy is tied up in action and not in self-doubt.

It's now time to move on to a vital tool for improving self-esteem: knowing how to take care of yourself. If you have found the last few sections challenging, sit back and enjoy. The next chapter is all about pampering yourself, relaxing and having fun. Now that's more like it!

CHAPTER 10

TAKE CARE OF YOURSELF

Another vital component of self-esteem is good health. If you feel ill, or tired or stressed, how on earth can you feel good about yourself?

If your self-esteem is low, you will almost certainly end up feeling unhappy and tired. You probably get ill a lot too. For some reason scientists and doctors don't yet understand – no doubt having to do with the mind-body connection and the fact that when you feel down you don't take such good care of yourself – with low self-esteem you are far more prone to illness, accidents and infections. When you feel good, you don't tend to get ill.

Poor health combined with low self-esteem is a recipe for disaster. You also increase the risk of slipping into depression, which is a harrowing and difficult illness. This chapter is all about secret number 6 to better self-esteem: taking care of yourself. As you read, try not to lose sight of the fact that you have responsibility for your well-being. The choices you make day-to-day affect your level of health and vitality. As much as possible, use the information here to make choices that support greater health.

BACK TO BASICS

The foundation stones for good health and improved self-esteem are eating right, exercising regularly, sleeping enough and having a network of support. The following guidelines should be enough to get you on the right track and boost your self-esteem at the same time.

SLEEP WELL

If you don't get enough sleep, you are more likely to feel irritable and anxious. Concentration will also be poor. Lack of quality sleep is one of the biggest causes of low self-esteem and stress.

You probably know the importance of a good night's sleep, but you probably don't know that there is no such thing as the right number of hours to sleep. Some of us get by with six hours, others need ten. We also need less sleep the older we get.

Everyone wakes in the night. This is quite normal. Most of us don't even realise it. It only becomes a problem when it prevents us from feeling rested. Everyone also has times when they don't sleep that well and sleep patterns are disrupted. This only becomes a problem if the disturbance is long term. Sleep is also affected by many things – what we eat, how much we exercise, how much we have drunk, what medications we are taking and so on.

So don't panic if you are not sleeping the required eight hours every night. Everyone has different sleep needs. The best indicator of sleep needs is how you feel during the day. Are you alert, energetic and able to concentrate? If you feel exhausted, irritable and like you are about to doze off all the time, you are not getting enough sleep.

It is possible to get a good night's sleep without resorting to medication. Drugs are not always that helpful and may even become addictive in the long term. Here are a few suggestions to help you sleep better.

■ Keep a diary. Record how much you sleep, but also record what you ate, how active you were and how stressful your day was. You may be able to identify unhelpful patterns that interfere with sleep.

- Relax before you go to bed. Take a warm bath or listen to soothing music.

- Avoid eating heavy meals two hours before you go to bed, but don't go to bed hungry. Perhaps a light meal in the evening would be best.

- Watch your stress levels during the day.

- Avoid caffeine (tea, coffee, chocolate and cola) late at night. A warm milky drink may help. Avoid alcohol, nicotine and spicy foods in the evening.

- Make sure your bedroom is comfortable and quiet. Use your bed for sleeping, not for reading and watching television. Your bed routines need to be associated with sleep.

- Go to bed when you are sleepy. If you take more than twenty minutes to get to sleep, get up and do something else until you feel sleepy. Do something that is simple and not too energetic, like light housework. Don't toss and turn worrying about why you can't sleep.

- Try to establish regular waking and sleeping times, even at the weekend. Long lie-ins don't really help until you have established a sleep routine.

Above all, don't worry about not getting a good night's sleep. Remind yourself that everyone has the odd night of poor sleep from time to time. In fact, recent studies show that getting too much sleep can be as bad for you as getting too little. Hopefully, if you follow these guidelines you should be able to establish a sleep routine. But if you still can't get a good night's sleep, it is important that you see a doctor.

KEEP ACTIVE

One of the most effective ways to boost self-esteem is to exercise regularly. It is almost guaranteed that you will feel better. When you exercise your body puts out chemicals, such as endorphins that can soothe a worried mind, as well as mood-enhancing neurotransmitters like serotonin. The hormones released during exercise affect your blood pressure, your heart rate, your body temperature, your metabolism. After exercise most of us feel happier, calmer and more alert.

As well as boosting self-esteem, exercise is also good in other ways. It will manage your weight, improve your health and reduce the risk of heart attack. It will also help you control aggressive emotions and help your mind to focus. It is an effective tool for treating depression.

You probably think you don't have enough time to exercise, but you don't really have time not to. Thirty or so minutes a day isn't really a huge chunk of time considering the enormous benefits. You don't have to join a gym or play sports if you don't want. A good exercise programme is one that you can do in your own home and one that improves your strength, flexibility and endurance.

As far as possible, ensure that exercise is a part of your life. Pick an activity you enjoy, and try to engage in some kind of physical activity every day. It can be as simple as walking home instead of getting the bus. The exercise should be moderate and not too intense. Too much exercise can strain your body and be as unhealthy as too little.

Something else that might help is the simple physical touch of others. A hand on your shoulder, a pat on the cheek or a massage can boost self-esteem. The act of sex itself can make you feel good. It can be a good form of exercise, can also stimulate the pleasure centres of the brain, be a stress reliever and release human growth hormone. Orgasm, whether it is achieved with or without a partner, sets off a chain of positive neurochemical reactions that should leave you feeling rejuvenated.

Stay sensual and you will have what Dr Michael Perring, quoted in *Ultra Age: Every Woman's Guide to Facing the Future* by Mary Spillane and Victoria McKee, calls a 'moist look'. Sensual people tend to look more confident and happy. There is always that sparkle in their eye. You may have a partner to keep sensuality in your life, but if you prefer to stay single make sure that you are surrounded by good friends and treat yourself to sensual pleasures, like a massage or a bubble bath, regularly.

Dancing is also a good treatment. When you combine music with exercise you have two powerful remedies. Music is one of the oldest treatments for anxiety. It's hard to feel bad about yourself when you listen to music you enjoy.

EATING TO BOOST SELF-ESTEEM

Most of us don't give our bodies the nutrition they need. If a machine isn't given proper fuel or maintenance, how can it be expected to run efficiently? Similarly, if you don't feed your body the full range of nutrients it needs, how can you expect to feel in top form?

Diet can play a role in boosting self-esteem. You may notice considerable improvements if you:

■ *Eliminate or restrict the intake of caffeine.* Chronic caffeine intake may cause worry and anxiety because it produces mental and physical stimulation. Caffeine in small doses can stimulate the brain and help you think more clearly and feel more alert. But the anti-fatigue effects of caffeine are usually short-lived. After the initial stimulation a period of increased fatigue results. A vicious cycle can be established when a person drinks more caffeine to delay the onset of more fatigue.

Caffeine is found in tea, coffee, chocolate and colas, and a small amount even appears in decaffeinated products. If a good cup of coffee is something you really enjoy, this doesn't mean you have to stop drinking it altogether; it just means you should cut down on the amount you drink. One or two coffees a day is fine, six or seven aren't.

Be aware that if you routinely drink coffee or tea, abrupt cessation will probably result in symptoms of caffeine withdrawal for a few days, and these include fatigue, headache and increased craving for coffee.

■ *Eliminate or restrict the intake of alcohol.* Alcohol interferes with normal brain chemistry and sleep cycles. In small doses alcohol can be calming, but more often it increases anxiety levels. If you suffer from low self-esteem, it is best to avoid alcohol entirely.

■ *Eliminate refined carbohydrates* from your diet. Refined carbohydrates, such as sugar and white flour, contribute to problems in blood sugar control and can promote hypoglycaemia, low blood sugar. When blood sugars are low the brain doesn't function well, and you feel anxious, dizzy and confused. Headaches may also occur. Simply eliminating refined carbohydrates from your diet may be all that is required to make you feel more confident.

■ If you regularly crave sweets, are irritable if a meal is missed, get dizzy spells or headaches, have problems concentrating, often feel tired or shaky, and suffer from mood swings and periods of confusion, try eating smaller, more frequent meals and adding protein to all your snacks. Reduce the amount of refined carbohydrates you eat, and consult your doctor.

Food and mood

Just when a balanced, wholesome diet is needed most, when your self-esteem is low you may neglect your body's needs. You may have no appetite at all, or you may crave unhealthy and fattening foods. As a result nutritional deficiencies or imbalances are likely. Malnourishment or weight problems clearly contribute to moods spiralling downwards. More and more research is linking what we eat to how we feel. In her book *Food and Mood*, dietician Elizabeth Somer explores how the food we eat can heighten depression. She believes that certain eating habits, like skipping meals or having erratic eating habits, aggravate negative moods. Somer advises five to six small meals and snacks spread throughout the day.

Dr Judith Wurtman, a researcher at the Massachusetts Institute of Technology, believes that certain foods alter mood because they release insulin, which encourages the production of serotonin. Higher serotonin levels are thought to be linked with improved mood. Foods rich in tryptophan, such as eggs, cheese, milk, peas and soya beans, and other foods rich in complex carbohydrates, have an effect similar to that of some anti-depressant medications. Somer advises that wholegrain breads and cereals or starchy vegetables such as potato or sweet potato can improve mood. She suggests that cravings are not to be avoided but responded to in moderation and with planned nutritious foods.

Designing a healthy diet

In general your diet should contain a balanced mix of carbohydrates, proteins and fats. You should also be eating enough fibre, ensuring that you get an adequate intake of essential vitamins and minerals, and drinking lots of water. Ignore all those celebrity high protein, low carb, cabbage, food-for-type, food-for-blood group, and so on diets. They are a waste of time. Focus instead on the guidelines given here which are in accordance with the Healthy Exchange System originally developed by the American Diabetic Association and other groups for diabetics, but now used for the design of many therapeutic diets.

Carbohydrate

The World Health Organization (WHO) and the Healthy Exchange System recommend that between fifty and seventy-five per cent of a person's diet should be carbohydrate. The carbohydrates should come not from foods high in sugar, like cakes and sweets, but foods rich in complex carbohydrates. Complex carbohydrates are high in fibre, low in starch and sugar, rich in vitamins and minerals and help keep blood sugar levels stable. Complex carbohydrates are found in bread, pasta, rice, potatoes, pulses, nuts and seeds, fruits and vegetables and salads.

■ *Best high-quality carbohydrate*

Fruits: apples, oranges, grapefruit, strawberries, pears, peaches and plums

Vegetables: broccoli, asparagus, green beans, cauliflower and spinach

Grains: barley, rye, brown rice, wholemeal and pasta

Beans: black beans, white beans, chickpeas, kidney beans and lentils.

You should have five servings of fruit, vegetables or salad a day and four servings of carbohydrates from other sources. A serving is one medium-sized apple and one medium slice of bread.

Protein

Protein should make up around fifteen per cent of your diet. Protein is found in meat, dairy produce, eggs, fish, poultry, pulses, nuts and seeds. You should try to have two servings a day of non-dairy products and one serving a day of a dairy product. A serving is two ounces of cheese or one egg.

Fat

Fats are found in most foods and are very high in calories. Too much of the wrong sort of fat is bad for you. Avoid saturated fats from animal produce and fats that are solid at room temperature, such as lard and butter. Fats that are liquid at room temperature, such as vegetable oils, are far preferable, since they don't contain the chemicals that can clog arteries.

Certain foods contain nutrients called essential fatty acids that are necessary for keeping insulin and blood sugar levels stable and are vital for a sense of well-being. Regular meals of cold-water fish such as herring and mackerel, as well as vegetable oils such as olive, sunflower and corn, and green leafy vegetables, are good sources.

Fibre

An adequate intake of dietary fibre is also important. WHO recommends around 30 g of fibre a day. Foods high in fibre include fruits and vegetables, brown bread, rice and pasta, high fibre cereals, potatoes and baked beans. A jacket potato contains around 5 to 8 g per serving.

Fibre swells the bulk of the food residue in the intestine and helps to soften it by increasing the amount of water retained. It is vital to the health of the digestive system, and many ailments, such as irritable bowel, constipation and piles, result if you don't get enough. Western diets are often low in fibre, and those who eat a lot of processed and refined food are vulnerable. But there are easy ways to boost fibre:

- Have a bowl of high-fibre cereal for breakfast.

- Eat brown bread, pasta and rice.

- Snack on fruits and nuts rather than crisps and chocolate.

High-fibre foods are nutritious and can satisfy without being fattening. Some types of fibre, those found in vegetables and fruits and oats, can reduce blood cholesterol. Cholesterol is a variety of fat that has some health benefits so it shouldn't be excluded from a diet, but too much cholesterol is linked to clogging of the arteries, especially those around the heart.

Vitamins and minerals

Vitamins and minerals are also vital for your health and sense of well-being. When there is a deficiency you may suffer from a range of health problems that undermine your well-being but are not normally treated by doctors. If you eat a wide variety of foods you should get all the nutrients you need. However, even fresh whole foods can be less nutritious than you think. Nutrients can be leaked from our food in a variety of hidden ways, and chemicals are often added.

Foods most at risk of nutrient deficiency are pre-prepared or processed food, foods that have been frozen and canned. In addition, alcohol, drugs, tobacco, stress and environmental pollution can deplete the body of essential nutrients. For all these reasons, you may want to try buying organic, eating as much fresh wholemeal food as you can, and supplementing your diet with extra vitamins and minerals.

■ *Common vitamins*

Vitamin A: Good for skin and eyes, found in liver, carrots and green vegetables

Vitamin B: Good for nervous system and circulation, found in bread, breakfast cereal, dairy products and vegetables

Vitamin C: Good for immune system and iron absorption, found in citrus fruits, vegetables, potatoes and green vegetables

Vitamin D: Good for bones and teeth, found in oily fish, salmon and dairy produce

Vitamin E: Good for fat metabolism and nervous system, found in nuts, seeds and vegetable oils

■ *Common minerals*

Calcium: Good for bones, teeth and blood clotting, found in milk, cheese and broccoli

Chromium: Good for sugar metabolism and blood pressure, found in egg yolk, wheatgerm and chicken

Copper: Good for healthy connective tissues, found in most foods

Iron: Good for blood, circulatory and immune systems, found in liver, dried fruit, meat and green vegetables

Magnesium: Good for muscles and nervous system, found in nuts, chicken and cheese

Potassium: Good for nerve transmission and acid/alkaline balance in the body, found in raisins, potatoes, fruits and vegetables

Selenium: Good for heart and liver, found in kidney, liver, red meat, cereals and brazil nuts

Zinc: Good for reproductive system, hair and nails, found in cheese, whole-meal bread and eggs

Vitamin A, C and E and selenium are anti-oxidants, which means they can help your body remove harmful toxins.

Warning: Always consult a doctor or pharmacist if vitamin or mineral supplements are taken. Some, vitamin A, for instance, can be harmful if taken in large amounts.

Water
The chances are you are not drinking enough water, an important

part of your diet. It keeps you hydrated and helps flush toxins out of the body. Ideally you should be drinking at least six to eight glasses of water a day to maintain health.

Salt and sugar intake

Moderation in salt intake is also advisable. Excessive salt intake can promote fluid retention and cause a rise in blood pressure and an increased risk of stroke, heart disease and kidney failure. Much processed food contains salt. Crisps are high in salt, and lots of us sprinkle salt on our food, which isn't necessary.

Refined white sugar is bad for your health. It rots your teeth, sends your blood-sugar levels up, affects your mood and makes you gain weight. Many of the foods we eat today are packed with hidden sugars, and most of us consume far too much. If you have a sweet tooth you might want to try eating fruit rather than sweets biscuits and cakes. Dried fruits especially can satisfy that sugar craving.

How much should I be eating?

If you follow the basic serving guidelines given above you should be eating a diet that is high in nutrients and sensible in calories. Calorie counting as a means of determining the healthful nature of your diet rarely works, because when you focus on calories you often neglect the importance of getting all your nutrients. A diet high in essential nutrients is far more effective in combating anxiety and stress than a calorie-controlled diet. You may find that a nutritious diet helps you lose weight more effectively too.

So forget calorie counting, and focus on nutrients.

When you eat

It seems that eating smaller, more frequent meals rather than larger, fewer ones is more beneficial for mental and physical health.

Breakfast is the most important meal of the day and ideally it should be the largest. Healthy breakfast choices include wholegrain cereals, muffins and breads along with fresh fruit, cereals, yoghurt, lean meat. The complex carbohydrates give you the energy boost you need at the start of the day. The protein will keep you from craving unhealthy snacks at mid-morning.

A light snack of fruit, vegetables, nuts or seeds around mid-morning will keep your energy levels high. Lunch is a good time to enjoy a nourishing bowl of soup or salad along with some wholegrain bread, lean meat, cheese or egg. This may be followed by another light snack around tea time.

Dinner should be the smallest meal of the day and preferably eaten at least two hours before going to bed. Wholegrains and legumes can be eaten in salads, main dishes and soups. It really doesn't make sense to eat a large meal when you are not going to need much energy. Give your body the time to rest, cleanse and recharge itself for the next day.

Daylight

Not getting enough sunlight can affect the way you feel about yourself, since sunlight is a source of nutrients. Simply go outside and get fresh air as much as you can. Even if it is cold outside and the sun isn't out, the light is good for you and will make you feel better. Don't take this to extremes, though. Too much sun can damage your skin.

SUPPORT FROM OTHERS

Positive relationships with other people help to build self-esteem. True self-worth can only come from within, but we all need to feel listened to, supported and reassured by others at times, however independent we are. Reassurance is the feeling that things will be all right in the end. A supportive statement from someone else can reinforce the supportive messages we've been giving ourselves. Children need reassurance and support all the time to boost self-esteem, but adults need it regularly too.

Sadly, in today's world many of us aren't very good at asking for help or giving it to others. We don't want to look vulnerable, needy or insecure. We ask for support in indirect ways, or we can't handle the responsibility of giving someone else reassurance. But if you ask for reassurance in a simple, honest way from someone you can trust, this can be very soothing.

Knowing that you have the support of other people is the ultimate form of reassurance. You don't need to ask for it because you know that others are supportive of you no matter what.

Unfortunately, when self-esteem is low you may not feel deserving of the support of others, and the sense of isolation makes you feel worse. So how do you go about regaining a sense of connection to others?

You could start by spending more time with your family and loved ones. The more connected you feel to the most important people in your life, the stronger you will feel. Schedule meals together. Talk more. Play more. Don't neglect your friends, either, and the ties you have with colleagues and neighbours.

Learning about your social and historical background may encourage a sense of belonging. So can staying current with information and ideas that are topical. You will feel more connected to what is going on in the world around you. Nurture positive connections at your place of work.

You might find solace and emotional connection by turning

to a higher source, perhaps through prayer or meditation. Talking to God, or if you are not religious to some higher source where you feel connected to the world, to nature, to time, to space, does seem to help. Research with brain scans shows that changes in the brain during meditation and prayer correlate with improved health.

In today's fragmented, fast-moving society it is hard to retain a sense of connection. Isolation and loneliness are modern epidemics. But it doesn't have to be that way. You don't have to feel lonely and isolated. Reaching out to those you know you can trust costs nothing and can be a source of great strength. Cultivating a network of social support could be the most healing thing you ever do for yourself. Friendship with people of both sexes is important. We need others to be happy, and to feel that we are accepted, and we need many kinds of relationships to feel loved and supported.

Don't forget, though, that although our lives find meaning through our relationships with others, how we feel about ourselves is just as significant. We need to feel loved and supported by others, but we also need to be able to love and support ourselves.

According to author John Gray, true contentment is only possible if we can meet all our love needs, both the love we give ourselves and the love we give others. In his book *How to Get What You Want and Want What You Have*, he outlines the ten essential love vitamins everyone needs in order to feel fulfilled: We need love and support from parents or carers, family, friends, peers and those with similar goals, ourselves, partners, and dependants. We also need to give back to the community, the world and to serve a higher source. 'A rich and satisfying life' is fuelled by these ten kinds of love and support.

Gray believes that when you don't feel happy or don't get what you want, it is because you are not getting your love needs met. 'Each of these different kinds of love and support is essential if we are to be whole.' We would all certainly feel better about ourselves if we loved and supported ourselves more and felt loved, supported and valued by others.

YOU ARE THE BEST FRIEND YOU WILL EVER HAVE

Secret number 6 is about taking care of your mental, emotional and physical health. Other people can lift your mood and support you, but ultimate responsibility for your health and well-being resides with you. If you saw your best friend neglecting their health, I'm sure you would be concerned and would encourage a change in attitude. Do the same for yourself. You are the best friend you will ever have. Take care of yourself.

CHAPTER 11

MANAGE STRESS

The ability to handle stress is secret number 7 to better self-esteem. Every time you feel you can't cope, or that you aren't good enough, a number of emotional and physical reactions occur that can trigger the stress response. If this response continues too long, the effects can be quite harmful.

Headaches, fatigue, aches and pains, depression, mood swings, irritability, upset stomachs, illnesses are all signs of stress. Low self-esteem can create stress, but the stress of various life events, such as death, debt and divorce, can also lead to self-doubt and confusion. Even when self-esteem is normally high, the stresses of modern life can throw you off balance. Everyone, however confident, can benefit from stress management techniques such as those mentioned below.

STRESS MANAGEMENT TECHNIQUES

The first step is to recognise the source of the stress. The more self-aware you become, the more you will be able to identify those areas of your life that are creating tension. Is your job too demanding? Are you unhappy in your relationship? As we suggested earlier, stand back and take an honest look at your life, and identify what is causing tension. If you can change the situation to ease the tension do it, but if you can't you need to learn new ways to manage stress.

Relaxation

Relaxation is the time when you recharge your batteries and focus on what makes you feel good. Unfortunately, many people with low self-esteem neglect setting aside time and space for themselves. When you are constantly anxious, muscular tension creates unpleasant sensations such as headaches, tightness in the chest, difficulty breathing, churning in the stomach, difficulty swallowing. These sensations trigger more tension, and a vicious cycle is set up.

It is important to learn how to relax in response to bodily tension. You may be able to do this by watching a movie or reading a book or listening to music or playing an instrument, but if you can't relax, you need to learn how to take time out. One way to do this is to relax your whole body slowly, muscle by muscle. Start by dropping your shoulders, relaxing the muscles in your body and in your face – it's amazing how many of us frown without knowing it – breathing deeply and gently relaxing. Many tapes on the market can help you through the process.

Techniques like meditation and yoga can also have astonishing results if you are stressed. Try this simple routine:

- Choose a focus word or phrase – for example, 'peace' or 'happy'.

- Sit quietly, and relax your body by tensing and then relaxing your muscles and breathing deeply.

- Say the focus word every time you exhale.

- If you lose concentration, simply return your thoughts to the word.

- Try this for just five minutes at first, and then gradually increase the amount of time.

■ Do the routine at least once a day.

Don't expect relaxation to be easy. If you are used to feeling tense, relaxing is a skill that has to be practised. If you feel uncomfortable at first, don't worry; just accept that it will take time. Make sure that you are breathing deeply and not practising when you are hungry, full or overtired. Make your environment conducive to relaxation. If you fall asleep easily, you might want to avoid lying down.

Expect your realisation to be interrupted by worrying thoughts. The best way to deal with them is not to dwell on them. Just accept that they will drift into your mind from time to time, and then refocus on your relaxation.

If you don't feel the benefit straight away, don't give up or try too hard. Just let the sensation of relaxation happen. Correct breathing will help.

Correct breathing

The way we breathe is important. Deep, slow breathing through the nose rather than the mouth while allowing your abdomen to move can calm both body and mind and help you cope with stress. Simple yoga breathing exercises, for example, breathing in slowly through the nose while counting to five, holding your breath for a count of five, breathing out slowly through the nose for a count of five, waiting a count of five and repeating as often as you like, may also help. Concentrating on breathing and counting can be wonderfully calming for your mind, while the regular breathing will calm the body.

When you are stressed you may hyperventilate or breathe rapidly. This rapid breathing is a natural response to stress or exertion. It uses the upper part of the lungs and results in too much oxygen intake. Rapid breathing isn't a problem if it is short term, but if it becomes habitual, it results in too much oxygen being taking into the bloodstream, upsetting the oxygen-carbon monoxide balance. Unpleasant physical symptoms can result, such as tingling of the hands or face, muscle cramps, dizziness, fatigue and aches and pains. These symptoms can be quite alarming, and they can trigger another cycle of stress.

It is easy to learn how to breathe correctly when you are anxious. Avoid breathing from your upper chest, and avoid gulping or gasping. When you first try to breathe correctly you may want to lie down to feel the difference between deep breathing and shallow breathing.

First exhale as much as you can. Then inhale gently and evenly through your nose, filling your lungs completely so that your abdominal muscles move outward. Then exhale slowly and fully. Repeat this, trying to get a rhythm going. You might want to aim to take ten breaths a minute. If you are not getting enough air, return to breathing that is normal for you. Then try increasing the length of one breath, breathing out fully, then in fully, then out again. If that breath felt comfortable, try another one. To get a rhythm going it's important not to try hard, but to cooperate as easily as you can with your breathing muscles.

It is important to practise correct breathing every time you feel stressed. As you practise, you will find that it gets easier and easier to breathe deeply instead of rapidly.

Relaxation techniques

In addition to the techniques for relaxing bodily tension discussed earlier, here are some more ideas for relaxing.

■ Imagery, a relaxation technique similar to daydreaming, involves allowing images to drift through your mind. Relax and let images come to you. Listen to tapes that induce relaxation without the sounds of nature or verbal directions; that way you can let your inner images flow freely. Such relaxation exercises done regularly can slow your breathing rate, calm your brain wave rhythms and lower your blood pressure.

■ Yoga can also relax tense muscles, teach you better breathing, lower your blood pressure, decrease your heart rate and divert your mind from stress.

■ Dr Gail Ironson, a professor of psychology and psychiatry at the University of Miami in Coral Gables, showed in a study that massage is vital for a stronger immune system and for reduced stress levels. Massage relaxes your muscles and gives you much-needed time out when you can revel in a feeling of being cared for.

■ Soothing music can be beneficial, as can soaking in a hot tub, laughing more, interacting with others, cultivating outside interests and diversions for your usual routine. There are so many delightful ways to relax.

Many of us think of relaxation as time we can't afford to lose. Rather than thinking of it as time lost, think of it as time gained. When you return to your routine you will feel refreshed and energised and feel better able to cope.

Time management

Not being prepared or organised can be a source of stress. Adding structure to your life can reduce time spent each day getting stressed about what you have forgotten, what you should be doing, and where things are. For example, if you are worried about being late, plan your journey and allow yourself enough time. If you worry about losing your keys, have one place where you put them.

Before you reorganise yourself take a look at your present routine, what your priorities are and what your goals are.

How are you using your time at work? How often do you procrastinate? You might want to write the details down in a diary. Once you become more familiar with the way you work, you can start looking at ways in which you can make the most of your working time. Organise your day. There will always be tasks you do on a routine basis and unplanned demands on your time, but try to create a definite plan for your day based on your goals and priorities. Tackle the hardest jobs first, when you have the most energy. Avoid putting things off until the last minute. You may find that you need to delegate some of your tasks. It might mean giving up things you enjoy, but it is faster to limit yourself to the appropriate tasks. Remember that delegation doesn't just mean passing on boring tasks. For others to be productive around you they need guidance, challenge and stimulation too.

In order to manage your time effectively you need to devise a system that meets your needs but that is also flexible. If you think you haven't got time to sit down and think about your schedule, remind yourself that time management is an investment that will pay off. You will feel calmer, better prepared, and more in control of your life.

And finally, don't be a perfectionist. Perfection is impossible to achieve. Do the best that you can, and then move on to other tasks. If you have time you can always come back later and polish the work more. An important part of time management is learning to compromise and rethink when necessary.

Specific stresses

Money, work and relationships can be causes of stress and low self-esteem. Let's look at ways you can minimise the risk.

Get your finances in order

There can be nothing more stressful and damaging to your self-esteem than the knowledge that you are spending more than you earn. Financial problems and debts can make even the most confident among us feel uncertain and nervous.

Money can't buy you happiness and self-respect, but financial stability can help you feel more confident and secure.

- Find out exactly what you spend your money on each week, and decide what isn't necessary.

- Set financial goals for a certain time period.

- Decide what you need to do to achieve those goals - reduce spending, increase income, work more hours and so on.

- Put your plan into action.

- If you can afford it, hire a financial planner to do your worrying for you.

A budget may be all that you need. This means setting up a system for allocating how much money you spend in each expense category based on what you have spent in the past. Determine your anticipated income, figure out your expenses categories, e.g. rent, tax, shopping, bills and so on, and determine how much you can spend in each category. Ongoing budgeting on a yearly, monthly or weekly basis can keep you informed of your spending habits and relieve a lot of worry.

If you do need to reduce expenses, review your current outgoings. Once you start thinking about your spending habits it becomes easier to cut out unnecessary expenses.

If you fear becoming destitute, do some research to find out what benefits you would be entitled to. Keep a file of this information for easy access. Think if there is anyone you could ask for support during a difficult time, and maintain strong connections with friends and family. Setting up a savings account may also bring peace of mind. If you are serious about reducing money worries, putting a little money aside each week can give you a feeling of security.

If your job is stressful

You may be in a job that is stressful, or you may feel that you aren't good enough at your job. You may feel that you will never get another job. A difficult boss or colleagues may be causing you a lot of stress. You may be putting up with a lot for the sake of that essential paycheck.

You can combat work-related stress by really thinking about what you want to do in your career. You might find that further education or study minimises stress and points you in the right direction. If you are tied to a job you don't like because you don't think you are good enough to do anything else, ask yourself one question: How do you know? How accurate is your self-assessment? Self-appraisal is hard to do, but it is important that you do it. List your strengths and weaknesses. You may surprise yourself.

If the problem is dealing with difficult co-workers, don't get sucked into a feuding war. Assertiveness skills will certainly help here and may be all that is required for the other person to back off. If he or she doesn't, speak to someone in authority in confidence about your concerns. If need be, consult with a lawyer. Remember too that in some way you might be contributing to the problem. Are you at times being difficult too?

One of the most powerful answers to work-related stress may well be increased togetherness and cooperation with others. Talk to the people you work with, involve them and don't get so wrapped up in your own work that you fail to recognise their needs.

If relationships are causing stress

Build your self-esteem by building positive relationships with others. Hopefully, your self-esteem will be high enough so that you don't spend time with people who are only interested in themselves or take you for granted. Also, if you believe that friendship is all about your needs being fulfilled, you are not a friend. Friendship is about giving and receiving and is based on the capacity to accept as well as to give love and respect. A good relationship with another person adds to your sense of zest and self-worth. If people sap your energy, you are mixing with the wrong kind of people.

It's impossible to go through life without meeting someone who makes you feel inadequate. Unfortunately, people with low self-esteem seem to be attracted to people like that, whereas people with good self-esteem seem to be successful in dealing with people who no longer enhance their lives and in seeking out those who do. This applies not only to partners but also to friendships and work colleagues.

Low self-esteem can be destructive in relationships. It can turn minor problems into major problems, and the insecurity of one person can affect another. This isn't a book about relationships so it's impossible to explore this subject in detail, much as I would like to. Let's just take a brief look at some typical issues.

If you are single, much depends on the attitude that you have towards your status. You can see it as liberating and a wonderful opportunity to develop your own interests, or you can see it as limiting, painful and lonely.

If you do not have a partner, there are things you can do to ease your loneliness and meet new friends and potential partners. You could do volunteer work, start a hobby, contact a dating service, network with friends and so on. But it is important to remember that a relationship is not the answer to feelings of low self-esteem and loneliness. Binding your self-worth to other people is a recipe for disaster. It makes you dependent and them resentful.

Once you feel good about yourself you will find that positive relating to others becomes much easier. You also give yourself a choice. You can choose to find a partner to enrich your life, or you may decide that you are just fine without one.

If you are a single parent, you can network and gather support from others in similar situations. You can also let go of what others think and focus on doing the best you can to raise the child or children that you love. If you don't know whether you should stay in a relationship for the sake of your children, get involved in counselling and make the happiness and well-being of your children your first priority.

Being in a relationship can be stressful. You may worry about the health of your partner, you may argue a lot with your partner, you may want more or less commitment with your partner. You may be jealous of him or her, you may fear losing your partner, you may feel resentment towards your partner, your partner may feel angry towards you or resentful of you. Whatever the case, don't ever think that a solution can't be found.

If your relationship is important, you will be willing to put a lot of time and energy into it to keep it strong and healthy. You might want to read books on relationships, attend workshops or attend counselling. Some of the strategies below may help:

- Engage in regular, open communication.

- Set aside regular time for each other.

- Do things together.

- Enjoy silence.

- Focus on what you love about each other.

- Give each other plenty of space to be who you are.

- Practise unconditional acceptance and love, but don't ever let someone else try to make you say or do things that you don't feel comfortable with.

If you are in an abusive relationship, these strategies may not be appropriate. Seek advice immediately from your doctor or a crisis centre.

Relationships with family members can also damage self-esteem. Children can be a great source of joy, but they can also be a great source of anxiety. Many parents simply aren't prepared for the huge change in their lives children bring. Parenthood can enrich and strengthen self-esteem, but it can also cause resentment, frustration and confusion. If parenthood gets rough, remind yourself that no parent is perfect. You are doing the best that you can.

Finally, friends and acquaintances can contribute greatly to the richness, enjoyment and security in your life, but if your self-esteem is fragile, the friends you have or don't have can enhance or damage self-esteem. You may worry about not having friends, whether or not people like you and what other people think of you. But there is a simple answer to such worries: if you want to have friends, be a good friend yourself. Be yourself. Be a friend, and you will have friends.

GETTING THE BALANCE RIGHT

In this chapter we have looked at secret number 7: managing stress. Stress often occurs when there is some kind of imbalance in your life. I'll conclude this chapter with the quickest and simplest technique to manage stress:

> *Always try to ensure that there is an even balance in your life between work, rest and play.*

We've already discussed the importance of rest and relaxation and getting a sense of perspective about work. But what about play?

CHAPTER 12

ENJOY YOURSELF

Secret number 8, enjoying yourself, is one of the best and most neglected ways to feel better about yourself. That's often the trouble with self-help programmes. Everyone takes themselves far too seriously. I've attended many self-help lectures and workshops in my time, and they are often conducted with the earnest solemnity you might expect at a memorial service.

The positive emotions associated with laughter decrease stress hormones and increase the number of immune cells. Think about all the things you really enjoy doing, and then try to work as many as possible of them into your life every day.

Research is now proving that pleasure does the immune system good. The more fun you have, the more gracefully you will age and the healthier you will feel. When we are happy, positive hormone and enzyme levels are elevated and blood pressure is normal. Even smiling can send impulses along the pleasure pathways to make you feel good. And besides, wrinkles from smiling are far more attractive than harsh frown lines.

Many studies have linked happiness to longevity and demonstrated that there are considerable health benefits in happiness and humour. It is important not only to find pleasure in your daily routine, but also to keep planning pleasurable activities in the future.

Many of us take ourselves far too seriously. Remember how

nervous and unsure you felt on your first date? Perhaps now you can look back you can look back with a smile. Have you ever thought that a few years from now you might look back and feel the same about what is worrying you at present?

Children laugh hundreds of times a day. Having fun and playing shouldn't stop just because you aren't a child anymore. Research shows that playing imaginative games can benefit concentration, coordination, attention span and general health and well-being. If you don't have enjoyment, laughter and fun in your life, then are you really living?

ENJOY THE WAY YOU LOOK

One of the biggest stumbling blocks many of us have when it comes to enjoying life is a poor body image. Feeling unattractive stops us living life to the full. Body image insecurity affects every aspect of our lives and is a major cause of fear, anxiety and depression.

So what do you do if you hate they way you look? The chances are that if you begin taking care of your body with the right diet and regular exercise you will start to respect and like your body more. But this won't happen overnight. In the meantime you have to stop trying to change your appearance and start trying to change the way you feel about how you look. Changing the way you think about yourself won't be easy. Be patient with yourself, and give yourself time. Take consolation from the fact that you are not alone and that you have to fight years of conditioning in the wrong direction.

Here are a few tips that may help:

■ Being thin does not improve your body image. I haven spoken to many people who had lost fat or who were at or below their ideal weight who still disliked their bodies.

- Spend some time really looking at other people your age. Notice how very different their bodies are from one another. Think about people you consider beautiful. Often their features are not perfect.

- Get to know your body better. Have a look at yourself naked in front of a mirror. Counteract negative thoughts about your body with something positive. Instead of 'I look fat', focus on how beautiful your eyes are, how good your hair looks, how great you look in a certain colour.

- Have a good long think about why you want to look different. Why is it so important to you?

- Listen to your body. Commit to trusting that it knows what it wants. Be honest about what you are eating. Make sensible, healthy food choices. Eat when you are hungry. Stop when you are full. Exercise when you can to help boost body confidence.

- If how you look is really making you depressed, seek professional help. You need guidance about how to change negative thought patterns, and a therapist might help. Call an eating disorder clinic at your hospital and ask for a referral. To keep you on track you might consider joining a support group that deals with food, weight and depression.

- Read some books on developing a healthy body image and self-esteem.

- Try to identify the real triggers for your body hatred. Every time you feel negative about your body think about what is going on at the time. Are you really angry with your partner? Has your boss upset you? Did you feel ignored by the shop assistant?

- Recognise that it is unnatural and unhealthy to look like the models on the catwalk. They are not real people but fantasies created by the media.

- Understand that thinness and youth do not equal attractiveness.

- Focus on what you are good at. Put your energy into doing things you enjoy.

- A positive body image makes a person attractive regardless of build or weight. Gaining this kind of body confidence starts with treating your body with respect.

- Rethink your definition of attractiveness. Beauty is not about youth and slenderness but about feeling confident about yourself. The sooner you come to this realisation, the happier you will be.

ENJOY YOUR WORK

Pleasure does not have to be separate from work. The ideal scenario would be that you found work that gave you a sense of vocation or pleasure, that you loved what you did for a living.

Being happy in your work means enjoying it as part of a balanced life. Research shows that if you have a sense of control over what you are doing at work, you will worry less and enjoy it more. This doesn't mean taking over the organisation. It means taking initiative and organising your routines as much as possible. If your job doesn't allow you this freedom, perhaps you should think about another working environment.

If you don't enjoy your work, do all you can to find an alternative. In the meantime, it might help to pretend that you do enjoy it, however boring and mindless the task, and to do it to the best of your ability. It may not be long before your enthusiasm is noticed and you are given the opportunity to do other work.

KEEP LEARNING

Your mind-set, not your appearance or your age, is what can hold you back. So take advantage of every opportunity that is offered to you. Keep pace with what is current. Continue to learn. Keep up with the gossip. Find yourself a mentor to inspire you. Stay in the mainstream.

And if you don't work, make sure that you love the life choices you have made, that you have friends, interests, hobbies, hopes and dreams. If you don't really enjoy your life and have at the moment no avenue of escape because of financial or family commitments, for your own sake find an interest that really motivates you. The important thing is to make the most of every day of your life. And if work is a large part of your life, you owe it to yourself to ensure that you use every day as an opportunity to learn, to grow, to be challenged and to enjoy.

STOP COMPARING YOURSELF WITH OTHERS

Comparing yourself with others is one sure route to low self-esteem. It's natural, of course, because we all have expectations of what we should be, what we should have accomplished, and many of us may feel that we have fallen short.

Everyone knows someone who is doing better than they and it's hard not to feel that you are lagging behind. But however beautiful, successful and talented your best friend is, he or she will have doubts of his or her own too. And there will always be people who are better than you in some things. That's just a simple fact of life.

The success of other people doesn't matter; what matters is how successful you feel you are. Other people don't have the same background, skills, and challenges as you have. Your life journey will never be the same as someone else's. Concentrate on your life, your skills, your talents and what makes you unique.

BE YOURSELF

Hopefully as you practise these new skills, self-confidence will gradually replace a vulnerable need for the approval of others. You discover that the important thing is whether or not you are being true to yourself. You don't need friends, parents or partners to validate your every action and thought. You begin to enjoy your own company and trust your own opinions. You start being yourself.

Only when you are yourself and you are happy to be yourself will self-esteem finally be yours.

The quickest way to improve your self-esteem is to be yourself.

Expect this to feel scary at first, but in time having the courage to be yourself and think your own thoughts is one of the most truly wonderful gifts that you can give yourself.

Find a place to be alone and enjoy your own company. Allow your thoughts to run wild. Rediscover dreaming and possibilities. Enjoy your *self*. Some of us find it harder to be alone than others.

But we are all born alone, and we all die alone. You are the only person who ever really knows yourself. No-one else can be inside you. You can see this aloneness as isolating and frightening, or you can see a wonderful kind of freedom. How you live is truly up to you.

And finally when you have the courage to be yourself, you will also find that you have the courage to 'let go'.

LETTING GO

Letting go doesn't mean not caring, it means not taking responsibility for what other people do, feel or think. It means allowing others to choose their own decisions and learn from their own mistakes. It means accepting that you are not all-powerful and can't always determine the outcome of events. It means not trying to change or blame others and making the most of yourself without putting others down. It means having the courage to look at your own shortcomings and trying to correct them. It means not criticising others but striving to be true to yourself and helping others to be true to themselves. It means living in the present rather than carrying the burdens of the past or worrying about the future. It means looking at the larger picture instead of being preoccupied with the details. It means loving others rather than trying to hold onto love.

You can do all you can to prepare yourself, you can try to make sense of your feelings, but it's impossible to be in control of every detail in your life. Sometimes you just have to put your doubts aside, take a risk and let go. You may make a decision, take some kind of action or simply change your attitude. Is this the best thing to do? You may never know, but at least you are seeking a solution and moving forward with your life.

Life finds its meaning through facing your fears, not by avoiding them. You can't always know if you are doing the right thing, but every time you search for an answer you add to your store of knowledge and life experience. Instead of letting self-doubt put your life on hold, you do what you were put on this earth to do: live, learn and grow.

IT'S UP TO YOU NOW

Improving your self-esteem isn't impossible. Apply the skills and techniques of the 8 secrets and you should be well on the way to replacing self-doubt with confidence and well-being. You will start to see that the quality of your life doesn't depend on what happens to you but on how you choose to react to it. It's been said earlier but it's so important I'll repeat it again: the choice is yours. Nothing that happens to you and nobody in your life can make you doubt yourself or your abilities without your consent. You can choose to doubt yourself and feel frustrated, or you can choose to be yourself and live life on your own terms.

BUT WHAT IF SELF-ESTEEM IS STILL LOW?

You are trying the techniques mentioned in this book, but you still don't like yourself much. What is going on?

You may just need more time. It takes a lot of practice to get the hang of new skills. If you have been feeling bad about yourself for a lifetime, you can't expect to instantly feel great. Don't give up, keep trying. Sometimes, though, low self-esteem may be a part of a more serious problem, such as depression. Low self-esteem is a symptom of depression and other mood disorders. If feelings of worthlessness and hopelessness persist, you may need extra help.

CHAPTER 13

EXTRA HELP, IF YOU NEED IT

If you feel you need extra help or advice, your first port of call is your doctor who can give you advice about various forms of medication, therapy, help and support available. Ideally any kind of medication, therapy or treatment should be used in conjunction with the self-help tips already mentioned. The useful addresses and suggested reading at the end of the book may also prove helpful.

MEDICATION

Medication won't give you your self-esteem back, but it can be an effective part of treatment. It can relieve symptoms enough to give you a ray of hope that recovery is possible.

Medications have side-effects, some of which are unpleasant. If antidepressant medication is an option, you will be informed of all the potential risks and benefits by your doctor. Remember too that they can only administered by a doctor, and a doctor will ensure the correct dosage for you and closely monitor your progress on them. You may need to experiment with various drugs to see which one is right for you. The mind is a mysterious thing, and it is impossible to predict with certainty which medication will be most beneficial to you. Don't give up if the first one doesn't work. The next one might. Let your doctor decide in consultation with you.

THERAPY

Psychotherapy broadly means 'talking cure', a client talking through problems with a therapist; but it's actually a term used for a wide range and scale of therapies and practitioners. For centuries therapy or talking about how we feel was the only option available. When done properly by trained therapists, therapy can work as well as medication. The secret is finding the right kind of therapy for you.

Many lives are enriched and repaired by therapy, but an unskilled therapist can be far more damaging than no therapist at all. If you need therapy you may feel in a vulnerable position, so it's important that your vulnerability is not exposed and exploited. If you are considering therapy and want to get something organised without first seeing a doctor, it's important that you are informed and educated about the different kinds of therapy available. Certification and licensing in various forms of therapy vary from region to region, so you need to exercise care in finding a therapist with adequate training.

Psychiatry

This branch of medicine is concerned with the diagnosis and treatment of mental disorders. A psychiatrist is a medical doctor who has done further training in psychiatry. Treatment usually involves a combination of drugs and therapy. It is important that you are aware that a psychiatrist is the only therapist who can prescribe drugs on prescription. Psychiatry is suitable for people with a recognised clinical depression or another mental illness such as schizophrenia.

Psychology

This branch of medicine is concerned with human behaviour. It is illegal for someone without training or qualifications to be called a chartered or licensed psychologist. Psychology is suitable for people with psychological distress or mental problems, including anxiety, phobias, obsessive compulsive behaviours, and addictive behaviour.

Many clinical psychologists work in private practice, but they are also found in health centres, hospitals and community centres. Counselling psychologists work with relationship problems and family issues. Education psychologists deal with children with emotional or social problems and learning difficulties. Occupational psychologists help companies with training, motivation and matters such as stress and workplace bullying.

While searching for a psychologist, look for the description 'chartered' or 'licensed psychologist'. The British Psychological Society publishes a register of chartered psychologists, and this is available at libraries or on their Web site. In the US contact the American Psychological Association to find out more about requirements for licensing, or call the state education department, division of professional licensing services, for the requirement of a particular state.

Psychotherapy

Traditional psychotherapy, called psychoanalytic psychotherapy, is the original talking cure. A client sits facing a therapist and discusses life problems. Each session takes an hour, and the treatment can last for months or years. It is based on the principles of psychoanalysis, placing importance on a patient's early life experience and exploring their thoughts, feelings, dreams and memories. The psychotherapist's skill is to listen carefully and to suggest new ways of seeing patterns or thought behaviour.

Psychotherapy is suitable for people with depression, anxiety, relationship problems, eating disorders, obsessive behaviour and low self-esteem. The aim of a good psychotherapist is to be a guide and support for you to find your own solution.

To find a psychotherapist look for accreditation from either the British Confederation of Psychotherapists or the United Kingdom Federation of Psychotherapists. Training takes a minimum of three years. The confederation also publishes two free pamphlets called *Finding a Therapist* and *Psychoanalytic Therapy*. The UK Council of Psychotherapy can inform you about qualified psychotherapists.

In the US there are no rules or restrictions about who can call themselves a therapist. If you are referred to someone who calls him or herself a therapist, be sure to ask questions about their psychological training to determine if they are suitable. In some states social workers are trained in psychotherapy. Check with your state authorities that the social worker is licensed and certified to be a psychotherapist.

It's impossible to describe all the various forms of psychotherapy in this book (for further information see Resources) but one form that is an effective tool for boosting self-esteem is cognitive-behaviour therapy, developed by a University of Pennsylvania psychiatrist, Aaron T. Beck.

Cognitive behaviour therapy
Cognitive therapy focuses on practical techniques; changing thought processes and behaviour to solve specific problems. It does not try to alter your moods; rather it tries to find ways of altering how you look at things that are causing your moods.

Cognitive-behavioural therapists believe that thoughts affect feelings and vice versa. The therapist would use this approach to help you focus on self-defeating automatic thoughts such as 'I'm a failure' and the unconscious belief system behind them. Negative thoughts are analysed as you would analyse the hypothesis of a scientific experiment. They are taken apart and tested bit by bit. Beliefs are explored together, tested, and finally changed.

For instance, if you think you are a failure, a therapist might ask, 'Are you a failure in every aspect of your life?' or 'Think of something you succeeded in doing last month.' The therapist helps you recognise for yourself that your thoughts may be illogical, distorted, one-sided, and faulty. When you are able to recognise this you can then start challenging negative thinking so that your feelings about yourself improve.

The work you do outside of the therapy session will be as important as the time spent in the session. You'll be given assignments each week. These assignments can consist of listing negative thoughts that occur during the day, reading material about anxiety, reviewing the therapy sessions on tape, writing, role playing and so on.

Brief therapy

Brief therapy refers to a combination of therapeutic techniques used over a short period of time. It often involves cognitive-behavioural techniques along with elements of analytical thinking or counselling. It is suitable for specific stress-related problems. The therapy is very goal oriented and practical. That doesn't mean, however, that there isn't an opportunity to explore feelings or past experiences.

Transactional analysis (TA)

Transactional analysis is a system of analysis and therapy

developed by Eric Berne (1910-1970). It has gained popularity because it is so simple and straightforward. TA places great emphasis on three selves, or 'ego' states: Parent, Adult and Child, normally abbreviated to P-A-C. The ego states are collections of all we have absorbed from significant others in our lives; parents, teachers, leaders and so on.

The Parent has two functions: the critical parent and the nurturing parent. The Adult state is analytical, rational and non-judgmental. The Child has two functions: the free or natural child, concerned with creativity, adventure and fun, and the Adapted Child who is angry, rebellious or conforming. Each ego state is accompanied by characteristic verbal and body language, voice qualities and feelings. We slip into and out of these ego states all the time in self-talk and in the way we relate to others. Problems arise when we respond inappropriately or can't understand or deal with an ego state in ourselves or in others. For healthy emotional development we need to find a positive balance between our P-A-C and to receive positive 'strokes' from ourselves and others.

TA identifies four life positions: I'm OK, you're not OK; I'm OK, you're OK; I'm not OK, you're OK; and I'm not OK, you're not OK. Obviously we need to aim for the I'm OK, you're OK position. The ways we tend to respond to problems, called 'life scripts' can be damaging because they repeat old patterns and don't allow for the possibility of creative change.

Transactional analysis is intriguing and can be incredibly insightful. It gets you looking at yourself and your reactions analytically and, as stressed earlier, self-awareness, recognising negative patterns and accepting your emotions are important stepping-stones on the way to improved self-esteem.

COUNSELLING

Counsellors often work in clinical or institutional settings along with other mental health professionals. There can be some confusion about the distinction between therapists and counsellors. Sometimes the difference involves qualification or training, but more often it refers to a different theoretical approach.

As a general rule counselling is shorter term and may be focused on particular issues that have arisen out of the past or present. It can enable a person to find solutions or insights into particular areas of his or her life. Counsellors are professionals who can help with emotional problems such as low self-esteem, loss, bereavement or addiction. During the course of the sessions a counsellor will help a person look at patterns of behaviour that are stopping him or her getting the most out of life. Sessions are just under an hour long and last for a period of time agreed between the client and counsellor.

Finding the right counsellor

In the UK a doctor can give you a direct referral to a counsellor. There may be one attached to the doctor's practice, or you may be given a list of available counsellors in your area if you decide to refer yourself. Usually counsellors who are attached to doctors' practices will see clients in a room attached to the surgery. You will probably be offered about six sections. Counsellors who are employed as part of a doctor's or GP's practice will have had their qualifications and references checked.

Finding the right counsellor may be a process of trial and error. They follow a range of theoretical backgrounds or 'models'. You may find this confusing at times, but you shouldn't be put off by wondering where they are coming from. At the heart of the counselling process is helping the individual. A counsellor is there to help you look at how problems are presenting themselves and to help you find a way through the difficulties you are facing.

Should you wish to go into longer-term counselling after the first set of sessions, you can ask about continuing, and if you need to look elsewhere the British Association for Counselling has lists of counsellors in local areas. There is also a reference directory on the Internet of qualified and registered practitioners.

Above all, check that the counsellor or therapist you visit is properly trained and qualified. The British Association for Counselling, and also the United Kingdom Council for Psychotherapists, can give further information and their addresses are at the back of the book.

In the US the term counsellor is used to describe a wide variety of different mental health professionals. They often work in clinics alongside other mental health professionals. Some counsellors hold a C.A.C., which means they are certified to counsel people on alcohol and drugs, but in most states no uniform licenses or certification are required to call oneself a counsellor. Check that the person has experience working with people who are mentally ill and a bachelor's or associate's degree in psychology, counselling or a related field.

WHAT DOES ALTERNATIVE MEDICINE HAVE TO OFFER?

Certain alternative remedies claim to be able to improve self-esteem, such as medical herbalism, nutritional therapy, autogenic training and Chinese and Ayurvedic medicine. They are best used alongside conventional therapy. Do check with your doctor first, if you want to try alternative medicine. The field isn't regulated, and although the majority of alternative therapists are authentic, you can also find unqualified, well-meaning but misguided practitioners.

NUTRITIONAL AND HERBAL SUPPORT

Nutritional and herbal support for the person with low self-esteem may involve supporting the adrenal glands – two small glands that are located above each kidney. The adrenal glands play a critical role in the body's resistance to stress. If stress is too great the adrenal glands will become exhausted and not perform well, causing worry, anxiety, fatigue, low self-esteem and depression.

Foremost in restoring or maintaining proper adrenal function is ensuring adequate potassium levels in the body – at least 3 to 5 grams a day. This is done by consuming food rich in potassium and low in sodium. A diet rich in fruits and vegetables should be able to do this. Foods rich in potassium include raisins, almonds, dates, carrots, mushrooms, garlic, dried figs and peanuts.

Should I take a supplement?

In an effort to increase our intake of essential nutrients, many of us take vitamin and mineral supplements. Medical opinion is divided on the use of such supplements. Some say that diet alone should provide all the essential nutrition, while others maintain that it simply isn't possible to get adequate intake through food alone.

Various studies have shown that our chances of consuming a diet that meets the recommended daily allowances (RDA) of essential nutrients are low, since most of us are too addicted to junk food. Better eating habits are the ideal, but for the majority supplements are advisable. This is especially the case if you suffer from stress.

The production of stress hormones tends to take priority over many other functions in the body which means that deficiency in certain key nutrients, such as vitamin B complex, vitamin C, magnesium and zinc are likely. If you are affected by stress, it is wise to increase your intake of foods rich in these nutrients but it would also be a good idea to take a good quality multivitamin and mineral supplement to compensate for any shortfall.

If you do decide to take a vitamin and mineral supplement, it should provide the full range of vitamins and minerals – all 13 vitamins and 22 minerals important for human function. Make sure that the vitamins and minerals are based on the RDA, or recommended daily allowances, prepared by the Food and Nutrition Board of the National Research Council. Bear in mind, though, that the RDA are designed to prevent nutritional deficiencies, and much remains to be learned about optimum intake of nutrients.

It is well known that during anxiety and stress vitamin C needs increase. Vitamin C is the ultimate anti-stress nutrient, yet because human beings are one of only seven species unable to make vitamin C, we have to consume it in our diet. When we are deficient in vitamin C our immune system and skin suffer, as vitamin C is necessary to make white blood cells and collagen. Extra vitamin C in the form of supplements (500 mg a day) along with an increased intake of vitamin C-rich food, such as all fruit and vegetables – especially citrus fruits, strawberries, cabbage and broccoli – is recommended.

When people are stressed they often lack energy. The B vitamins are involved in the production of energy. You need to replenish B vitamins daily and bear in mind that their supply is reduced by refined goods, alcohol, sugar and coffee. You can find B vitamins in wholegrains, green leafy vegetables, liver, dates, figs, legumes, cauliflower, broccoli, salmon, yoghurt, tuna and tomatoes. It is best to take B vitamins in their complex form but vitamin B3, B5 and B6 are very important. Take 50 mg of multi-B complex daily.

Magnesium plays a crucial role in the manufacture of stress hormones. Stress induced muscle twinges and cramps as well as migraines, high blood pressure and depression are often related to an imbalance between levels of magnesium and calcium. Food sources of magnesium include green leafy vegetables, fresh seeds and nuts. 250 mg magnesium balanced with 250 mg of calcium can help to redress insufficient magnesium levels. Do not take if you are on calcium blocking medication.

Zinc is depleted by a stressful lifestyle and many of us are deficient. Signs of deficiency include white marks on the nails, pale skin, stretch marks, loss of libido, frequent infections and depression. Food sources include seeds, lentils, oysters, wholegrains, seafood, nuts, lean meat and green leafy vegetables. 10–15 mg daily can be a useful boost.

The human body and mind can't function well without essential fatty acids. There is growing evidence that many people, especially women, suffer from a deficiency of omega-3 oils, a type of essential fatty acids. Deficiency in essential fatty acid is linked to dry skin and nerve disorders.

Regular meals of cold-water fish such as herring and mackerel and seafood provide enough omega-3, but you may need to take fish oil capsules. Your best source of high-quality flaxseed oil, a rich source of essential fatty acids, will be a health food store. It is best to take the oil in liquid rather than capsule form. Other popular vegetable oils, such as olive, sunflower and corn, contain essential omega-6 oils. Green leafy vegetables are another good source.

Plant-based medicine

Various herbs support adrenal function. Most well known are the ginsengs. Chinese Panax ginseng and Siberian ginseng can enhance the ability to cope with stresses, both physical and mental. Research shows that ginseng offers significant benefit to people suffering from anxiety and fatigue. Ginseng, particularly Panax ginseng, can restore adrenal functioning for individuals under extreme stress. Panax ginseng is generally regarded as more potent than Siberian ginseng. If you have been under chronic stress and constantly feel anxious, Panax ginseng is advisable, but if you have been under mild to moderate stress, Siberian ginseng may be your best choice.

Many types and grades of ginseng extracts are available, and each individual's tolerance to ginseng is unique. It is advisable to consult with a qualified herbalist to establish the dose that is right for you. Too much ginseng, or the wrong kind of ginseng, can produce unpleasant symptoms and increase anxiety levels.

The adrenal glands can also be supported by taking oral adrenal extracts, which are made from beef.

St John's wort

St John's wort, or *Hypericum perforatum*, is a herb that is widely used and prescribed in Europe for depression. It is emerging as one of the most popular, effective and safest antidepressants – perhaps even more popular than conventional antidepressants. For example, in Germany it is the number one antidepressant prescribed by doctors, far outselling Prozac. Every year German doctors write three million prescriptions for it, as compared with 240,000 for Prozac. It could become an astonishing alternative or adjunct to the drugs now used in the US and the UK to treat depression.

St John's wort is a naturally occurring herb, not the result of pharmaceutical development. It does appear to help many people suffering from depression, with minimal side-effects. It can also help reduce the symptoms of anxiety and stress. Research on St John's wort is still in its infancy, but recent studies show that it may affect the transmission of all the neurotransmitters serotonin, norepinephrine and dopamine, which are thought to create a feeling of well-being.

The target dose in most antidepressant studies of mild to moderate depression is 900 mg of Hypericum a day, and the Kira TM brand is most often recommended. Side-effects are rare, but may include stomach upsets, fatigue and less commonly allergic reactions. It can also occasionally interact with other drugs, so you need to ask the pharmacist or your doctor for advice before starting to take it. It's perhaps best to start with a lower dose and build up, but self-medication is a tricky business. Each person will react differently. St John's wort is being hailed as a wonder drug by some enthusiasts, but it is important not to put all your hopes in one treatment alone and to keep an open mind. Some people don't feel better after taking it.

Being properly informed is crucial. You will find information about the herb in books about the medicinal properties of herbs. Dr Norman Rosenthal's *St John's Wort: Your Natural Prozac* is an invaluable guide that will tell you everything you need to know about the herb, how it can help, how to take it, what the side-effects are, and how to monitor progress on it.

Warning: St John's wort should not be taken alongside certain medication or the contraceptive pill. It can also increase sensitivity to the sun. Seek advice from your doctor.

Kava

In the Islands of the Pacific, Kava is a drink made from Kava root. It is used for its calming effect and its ability to promote sociability in the Islands of the Pacific. Preparations of Kava root are now gaining popularity in Europe and the USA for their mildly sedative effect.

Kava drinkers say they experience a pleasant sense of tranquility and sociability and a reduction in anxiety. If you take standardised Kava extracts at recommended levels there should be no side-effects. High doses are unnecessary and should not be encouraged. Always follow the therapeutic dosage recommended, which is usually between 135 and 210 milligrams daily. In time you may feel more optimistic and have a relaxed mental outlook.

OTHER REMEDIES THAT MAY HELP

The therapies listed here all adhere to the principle of holism: the body, mind, spirit and emotions are interdependent parts of the whole person. If you lack confidence in yourself, practitioners of these therapies will want to build up a picture of your whole life and your unique constitution.

Alexander technique

This is a system of re-education aimed at helping you regain natural balance, posture and ease of movement and to eliminate habits of slouching or slumping. You will be taught new ways of using your body and new ways of keeping your spine free of tension. The Alexander technique can help with stress-related conditions, including fatigue and anxiety. The anxious tensing of muscles can contribute significantly to feelings of low self-esteem. Confidence can be boosted when you stand tall and relaxed with your head high.

Aromatherapy

Aromatherapy involves the use of oils extracted from plants, herbs, and trees to promote physical and emotional well-being. It is often used in conjunction with massage. Oils can be rubbed into your skin or added to your bath. Oils most often recommended for anxiety are sandalwood, chamomile, lavender, rose, clary sage, lavender and bergamot.

Autogenic training

You might consider autogenic training, a gentle form of self-administered psychotherapy that teaches special mental exercises to help you relax mentally and physically and replace negative thoughts with positive ones.

Ayurveda

Ayurveda is the name of the Indian science of life. It is a comprehensive health-care system and incorporates detoxification, diet, exercise, breathing meditation, massage and herbs. Herbs are used as part of remedies designed to correct different sorts of energy imbalances in your body. Anxiety is believed to be a symptom of such imbalances, and an important aim of the skilled practitioner is to eliminate them. Yoga can be a significant part of ayurveda.

Bach flower remedies

There are thirty-eight different flower remedies, all widely available in chemists and health stores. The remedies are good for balancing emotional, spiritual and psychological states such as uncertainty, indecision and despondency. Bach Rescue Remedy combines the benefits of several flowers and acts as a quick boost when you feel low.

Chinese medicine

Acupuncture and herbalism form the basis of traditional Chinese medicine, a system of health care still widely practised in Hong Kong, China and in some states in the US. Herbs are used to prevent ill health and to treat both mental and physical illness and to balance emotional upset. Ginseng is a well-known Chinese remedy to stimulate energy. Tiger balm is used to relieve aches and pains.

A doctor of Chinese medicine will recommend the herbs that address the particular imbalances in the patient that are contributing to low self-esteem. Because the effects are gentle, improvement is seen after several weeks or several months of treatment.

Acupuncture involves using needles to stimulate points in the body called acupoints. Over thousands of years the Chinese have mapped the network of energy lines that permit the flow of vital energy through the body. In the Chinese system, anxiety causes or is caused by blockages in these energy lines. An acupuncturist relieves the blockage by stimulating select points. Those who have experienced acupuncture report feeling calmer and more clear-headed after treatment.

Acupressure is a form of massage built on the philosophy of acupuncture. In acupressure the acupoints are stimulated to alleviate depression. Pressure points associated with anxiety include a point four fingers' width from the inside of the ankle and a point two fingers' width from either side of the spine, just below the shoulder blades.

Herbalism

Medicinal herbalism uses the curative properties of various parts of plants, such as flowers, trees, bark, nuts, seeds and herbs, to maintain good health and treat disease. Herbs can be taken in a variety of forms – tinctures, teas, infusions, creams, ointments, or capsules. St John's wort is one such herb.

Warning: Many natural remedies, such as herbal preparations, are available at chemists and health stores, but self-medication is not usually advised and you should always consult a qualified practitioner. Make sure also that you check with a doctor that the medications are safe and do not interact with any current medication.

Homeopathy

The art of treating like with like, homeopathy relies on the belief that a substance that causes particular symptoms can also be used in minute doses to cure those same symptoms. Remedies are derived by diluting, in water and alcohol, sources taken from plants, minerals and animals. Homeopaths prefer to treat each case individually, but *Natrum mur* is often recommended when a person thinks constantly of past, sad events. *Ignatia, Pulsatilla* and *Sulphur* may also help lift mood.

A special homeopathic combination, *L.72 Anti-Anxiety*, has been shown to be effective in treating anxiety.

Hypnotherapy

Hypnotherapy can be a powerful aid for those fighting addictions to alcohol, cigarettes or drugs, for those suffering traumas or phobias, and for those wanting to boost self-image. A hypnotherapist can induce a light trance in the client, which can bring to consciousness repressed emotions. This is particularly helpful in the case of depression. The client becomes receptive to suggestions that can help him or her accept or reject patterns of belief or behaviour, also helpful for depression. In unskilled hands hypnotherapy may be unwise, so make sure a therapist is chosen carefully.

Meditation

Meditation or visualisation are contemplative techniques that can calm and clear an overactive mind. During meditation brainwaves change to a distinctive pattern linked with deep relaxation and mental alertness. Regular meditators can shift into this mode at will, allowing them to deal efficiently with stress.

It is one of life's ironies that those who would benefit most from meditation are invariably the ones who are most resistant to it. If self-esteem is low, you may feel too anxious to try meditation or it may not appeal to you, but studies show that it can boost self-esteem.

Nutritional therapy

Nutritional therapy uses diet and vitamin and mineral

supplements to balance the body and prevent illness. There are three basic diagnoses: food intolerances, nutritional deficiencies and toxic overload.

A nutritional therapist analyses samples of blood, sweat or hair to detect deficiencies. Low self-esteem has been linked to low levels of serotonin. Serotonin is made from the amino acid tryptophan, and for the body to convert tryptophan into serotonin, vitamins B3, B6 and zinc are essential, so levels need to be kept up. A diet high in complex carbohydrates is recommended. Naturopaths suggest eating turkey, nuts, milk and bananas, as they contain tryptophan.

Toxic overload is diagnosed through an analysis of symptoms and diet, and fasting may be recommended to clear the system. A diet high in sugar and saturated fats, such as hamburgers and french fries, can lead to fatigue and depression. Alcohol, caffeine and processed foods, as well as smoking, deplete the body of essential nutrients and increase the risk of anxiety.

Soothing therapies

Soothing colours can be a good antidote when you feel anxious; they work by calming the activity of overstimulated brain waves. Colour therapists often recommend blue to encourage clear thinking and feelings of serenity and healing, orange to keep the spirits up when they are low, yellow for optimism and creative confidence, red for energy, green for healing and balance, pink to link with nurturing qualities and purple for looking inward.

Music can uplift and inspire. Whether it's Mozart or Madonna, music can soothe a troubled mind. But music does more than uplift, inspire and soothe; regular rhythms and tonal structures can elicit suppressed feelings in need of expression and catharsis.

Tai chi and yoga

Tai chi is a gentle art that employs meditation and calm, smooth dance movements to improve the health of mind, body and spirit. Breathing should be coordinated with movement. In order to make a significant difference to health, tai chi needs to be practised regularly.

Like tai chi, yoga pays attention to breathing and incorporates meditation. Yoga poses keep the joints and muscles flexible, build strength and promote health through nourishing the internal organs with breathing and movement. Salutary effects on the immune system have also been attributed to it.

If you want any further information on any of these therapies, or others not listed here, you should contact the Institute for Complementary Medicine (see page 132) which is an impartial organisation that acts on behalf of consumers of natural medicine as well as promotes research into the safety and effectiveness of alternative therapies.

Don't forget this book!

In this chapter we've looked at ways you can get extra help if you think you need it, but in most cases you can improve self-esteem without seeing a doctor, taking pills or supplements or going on yoga retreats. This book gives you all the information you need to help yourself. Carry it with you at all times as a source of comfort and reference when doubt strikes.

CHAPTER 14

CONFIDENCE-BOOSTING TIPS

The eight secrets recommended in this book are simple and easy to apply, but simple doesn't mean quick. You can't change the habits of a lifetime in the time it takes to read this book. Learning new habits takes time and practice. Healthy self-esteem doesn't happen overnight. Don't give up if you don't get immediate results.

If you keep working on the skills outlined in this book, you will begin to notice positive changes. Change often begins in a small way; in fact, you may hardly recognise it. You may have doubted yourself for so long, and then suddenly one day a spark of confidence is rekindled.

And while you are working on the skills that can lead to lasting improvements in the way you feel about yourself, you might find some of the confidence-boosting suggestions in this chapter helpful.

THE CONFIDENCE HABIT

People with self-esteem have confidence. Confidence is believing in yourself and being relaxed and secure in the company of others. It is doing what you want to do, when and how you want to do it. It is being comfortable with yourself and not worrying what others think. Confident people feel secure in the knowledge of their talents and are keen to listen to and learn from others. Remember that confidence should not be confused with arrogance, which is often a defence used by those lacking confidence to protect their profound insecurity.

Confidence is a natural force within you, and with a bit of self-awareness and skill it can become a habit. If you can think of lack of confidence as an annoying habit, like biting your nails, you will realise that you can do something about it. Practise the skills in this book to build self-esteem whenever you lack confidence and feel insecure. Start replacing the habit of self-doubt with the habit of confidence.

FIRST IMPRESSIONS

First impressions, how you carry yourself and how you communicate, count. Most people tend to judge you on first impressions.

Body language and non-verbal cues are crucial in terms of your impact on others. For instance, do you typically stare at the floor or avoid eye contact? This will make you look not only nervous but also uninterested, which can lead people to ignore you. Posture is also important. When frightened, humans tend to want to shrink. It's obvious that if you walk tall, straighten your spine and look someone in the eye, you will appear more confident.

It also helps to avoid nervous fiddling movements with your body, hands, feet or face. Gestures are good things; they can add emphasis to what we say, but folded arms or unnecessary fidgeting can make you look defensive or very anxious. Touching others when appropriate, a handshake when you meet, for instance, can also help build relationships and put another person at ease. Do be respectful of a person's privacy and personal space, though. It's intimidating if someone tries to get too close.

It can be helpful to watch yourself in a social situation on a video camera. Try it and see what areas you could improve on. Relaxation techniques can also be useful. Another great technique is simply to imagine you are someone very confident, such as Julia Roberts or Richard Branson, and imagine how they would behave. Then go on to practise this in the real world.

WRITE IT DOWN

Writing can be therapeutic. Write the story of your life. Write about the significant people, events, successes and set-backs in your life. Try to focus on what is positive. Try to think about how past events influenced your self-esteem. This may be painful, but the pain is healing. Building self-esteem begins with understanding yourself. If you can find the positive in the past, then the past isn't controlling you anymore.

You could also make a creative journal, which records everything you want from your life. Be realistic and honest with yourself. Ask yourself how, in an ideal world, you would like your life to be in terms of your relationships, career and home. Read your journal regularly and don't let go of your dreams. Once you know what your goal is, start making it happen by talking and thinking about it.

AFFIRMATIONS

The mind listens to what you tell it. If you constantly tell it you are worthless, you can't cope or people won't like you, it believes it. It's time now to give your mind a new script. Faulty self-talk lowers self-esteem like nothing else. Positive self-talk boosts self-esteem.

At first it will seem strange telling yourself you can do it, you're good enough, and so on, but keep trying. You need to believe you can change for change to happen.

BE ENERGETIC

Human beings are meant to be full of energy. One of the most distressing consequences of low self-esteem is that you tire easily. Take regular exercise. Don't sit around so much. Generate mental energy by thinking positively, managing your time and making your own decisions. Kill boredom by keeping your mind stimulated, being creative and showing an interest in others. Make sure you get a good night's sleep and avoid stress. Practise relaxation techniques. Don't let negative emotions such as anger, guilt and anxiety gain an upper hand. Working towards your goals will encourage others to feel good about themselves. Energy is contagious.

ORGANISE YOURSELF

Perhaps you could organise your self-esteem building skills around a weekly timetable, a self-esteem-boosting schedule:

- Sunday is the day of the sun – the healer and bringer of light. It is a day to work for *self-healing*. Use this day to take better care of yourself, physically, emotionally, spiritually and mentally. Focus on your strengths and not your weaknesses. Remind yourself that you don't need to be perfect.

  Thought for the day: *'You must feel love for yourself before you can give love to others.'*

- Monday is the day of the moon – the world of feelings and

intuition. It is the day to try to make sense of what your feelings are telling you.

Thought for the day: *'Self-knowledge is the beginning of wisdom'.*

■ Tuesday is the day of Mars – the warrior. It is the day to talk to yourself with *courage*, strength and determination. Learn to talk to yourself constructively. Balance old patterns of automatic negative thinking whenever you can with positive ones. View problems and change not as obstacles but as challenges.

Thought for the day: *'Your mind believes what you think, so think success and not failure.'*

■ Wednesday is the day of Mercury – the messenger of the gods. It is the day to *reach out* to others. Focus today on improving your communication skills and making connections with others. Gather support from friends, family, partners, colleagues. Talk about how you feel to people you can trust. Ask for their help, reassurance, advice and support.

Thought for the day: *'There is nothing wrong with asking for help.'*

■ Thursday is the day of Jupiter – whose power is that of expansion and growth. Use this day to take action and make positive changes in your life.

Thought for the day: *'Achieving a goal means being clear about what that goal is.'*

■ Friday is the day of Venus – whose power is love and harmony. Use this day to focus on *love*, harmony and partnership. Cherish the very special people in your life, remembering that to win the love, friendship and respect of others you must give love, friendship and respect yourself. And don't forget to cherish yourself and your life too.

Thought for the day: '*You teach others how to treat you*.'

■ Saturday is the day of Saturn – the planet of wisdom and insight. Today is the day to *learn and let go*. Use this day to consolidate all that has been gained, reflect on advances made, learn from set-backs and revise your plans for the future in light of what you have learned about yourself. Today is the day to remind yourself that although you can't always choose what happens to you, you can always choose how you react to it.

Thought for the day: '*It's up to you what kind of life you lead*.'

REMEMBER THE GOOD TIMES

On those days when you feel that nothing is going right, pause for a few seconds and think of a time when you felt happy, cared for and loved. Anything that gives you a memory of success. It may be when your children were born, when you passed your driving test, when friends gathered for a birthday. It doesn't matter what it is, just think about it for a while to remind you what it is like to feel good.

However ghastly you feel, something good can always be found in your life. A key element in self-esteem is a feeling of belonging. Think of all the people who rely on you and whose lives you touch in big or small ways. It could be the old woman you held the door open for or a friend who has been very supportive. Another key element in self-esteem is appreciating what you have. It's a cliché, but if your health is good you already have the most wonderful gift life can give you.

PAMPER YOURSELF

Take time each day to pamper yourself. Treat yourself to a warm bath, cook yourself a special dish. Take care of your body, and it will take care of you. Take time out and allow yourself time to relax so that you can become more productive and energised.

It also helps to make your surroundings more pleasant and relaxing. It's amazing how much a bunch of fresh flowers or an interesting picture can inspire you.

REINVENT YOURSELF

Dare to be different or do something you haven't done before.

It's easy to get stuck in a rut and do things because you have always done them that way, but you don't have to. Something as simple as a new haircut or a change of wardrobe may be all that you need to give yourself a quick boost.

MEET YOURSELF

Sometimes when you feel down, you might wish for someone to come along and help you feel better. As a matter of fact you do know someone. It's you.

It might be helpful for you to imagine that you have an inner guide who wants to help you and show you a path to self-acceptance. Take the time to meet and talk to that inner guide. He, she or it has so much to tell you. In meeting your inner guide you are meeting your own wisdom and goodness. Your inner wisdom is always available, and you can call on this figure whenever you need a shot of self-esteem.

REFRAME PERCEPTIONS

Stop making black-or-white judgments. Life is far too complex to be rigidly divided this way. If ever you start thinking that you have totally messed up or that everything went wrong, remind yourself that nothing is 100 per cent bad.

Stop judging yourself and others. We're all doing the best we can. Don't waste time and energy with negative attitudes. Spend a day looking for the positive in yourself and others. Give compliments to others, and accept compliments if they are given to you.

If you tend to focus on the negative it is time to look for more balancing positives in a situation. Avoid global generalisations such as stupid, ugly, failure, total disaster. These are just labels; they're not the whole story. And finally, stop trying to read minds. How do you know what other people think? How do you know what other people will do? Don't ever assume anything.

Here's a little exercise:

List three things about yourself you like and then three things you don't like. Do the same for a friend or a famous movie star.

This exercise shows you how easy it is to tilt your reactions and feelings simply by choosing to focus on different sets of facts.

FIND COMPASSION

We all have emotional wounds inflicted upon us by others. It's easy to feel resentful and angry, but as long as you feel anger and resentment that person is still controlling you. Don't give them that power. Let the hatred go, and let the hurt inflicted upon you fade from your life.

Find compassion for the people you have upset. If guilt is holding you back, try to get understanding, forgiveness and acceptance from the person you have hurt. If that isn't possible, imagine that person forgiving you.

Find compassion for yourself. It's hard to feel love and compassion for others if you can't love and feel compassionate for yourself. Stop kicking yourself. Look for ways you did your best, and give yourself credit for making the effort.

With the exception of children under eighteen you are not responsible for the thoughts, feelings and actions of other people. Keep reminding yourself of that. Spend time with people who uplift and inspire you, and stop associating with the negative ones.

The only person you should feel responsible for is yourself. Self-esteem can be greatly enhanced when you accept responsibility for making your own decisions and have the personal commitment to carry them through. Achieving your goals is a satisfying boost to self-esteem.

LITTLE THINGS

Many things we think are insignificant can make a huge difference. Finishing an uncompleted task, having a spring clean or a tidy up, writing a letter to someone you care about, reading an inspirational book, helping others, a trip to the cinema are all ways to improve the way you feel about yourself. Basically anything that you enjoy doing and that gives you a feeling of achievement is an effective boost to self-esteem. Find what works for you.

DON'T LET SELF-ESTEEM DEPEND ON OUTWARD SUCCESS

Having money in the bank can lift your spirits, but if self-esteem isn't good the lift is temporary. It's not difficult to find examples of the famous and rich who are terribly unhappy and unfulfilled.

A study conducted by psychologists at the University of Missouri, Columbia, in early 2001 concluded that money really doesn't buy lasting happiness. Instead, happiness comes through being true to yourself, having close bonds with other people, respecting yourself and feeling competent at activities.

If you find that you are becoming too dependent on outward show, this little poem can always help put so-called success in perspective.

> At age 4 success is not peeing in your pants.
> At age 12 success is having friends.
> At age 16 success is having a driver's licence.
> At age 20 success is having sex.
> At age 35 success is having money.
> At age 50 success is having money.
> At age 60 success is having sex.
> At age 70 success is having a driver's licence.
> At age 75 success is having friends.
> At age 80 success is not peeing in your pants.

Real success isn't about appearance, friends, money, what you have or what you do, it's about being true to yourself and leading the kind of life you want to lead. It's about having self-esteem.

AFTERWORD

You may not realise it, but you are a success already. At conception a million and one things could have happened to prevent the embryo that would later become you being born. What makes you even more incredible is that you are totally unique. There has never been and never will be any one like you again. You are one of a kind. Only you can make the contribution that you came here to make.

The only person who can make you feel bad about yourself is you. If you have learned just one thing from this book, I hope it is that. However dark and difficult things get, however much you feel rejected or criticised, you don't need to feel bad about yourself.

Confidence in yourself comes from the thoughts that you have about yourself. Everything begins with your thoughts. You are what you think. If you choose to think positively about yourself and your life, you experience feelings of enjoyment, energy and satisfaction. If you choose to think negatively about yourself and your life, you experience feelings of dissatisfaction, fatigue, and uncertainty.

If you can think about yourself in a positive way, if you can find the courage to be yourself and to celebrate your uniqueness, then you will discover amid the routines, the struggles, the set-backs and even the moments of great pain that you are wonderful just as you are. It's often hard to see this, but it is true.

Never forget that, just like the trees and the stars, you have a right to be here. Be yourself, believe in yourself, take care of yourself and strive to be happy.

READING GUIDE AND USEFUL ADDRESSES

SUGGESTED READING

Carlson, Richard, *Don't Sweat the Small Stuff*, Hodder & Stoughton, 1997

Carnegie, Dale, *How to Enjoy Your Life and Your Job*, Pocket Books, 1985

Chopra, Deepak, *Seven Spiritual Laws of Success*, Amber-Allen Publishing and New World Library, 1993

Chopra, Deepak, *Ageless Body, Timeless Mind*, Harmony, 1993

Covey, Stephen, *The 7 Habits of Highly Effective People*, Simon & Schuster, 1990

Dyer, Wayne, *Your Erroneous Zones*, Warner, 1992

Field, Lynda, *Creating Self Esteem*, Vermilion, 1993

Goleman, Daniel, *Emotional Intelligence*, Bloomsbury, 1996

Gray, John, *How To Get What You Want and Want What You Have*, Vermilion, 1999

Harris, Amy, *Staying OK*, Arrow Books, 1995

Harris, Thomas and Amy, *I'm OK – You're OK*, Arrow Books, 1995

Hay, Louise, *You Can Heal Your Life*, Eden Grove, 1988

Jeffers, Susan, *Feel the Fear and Do It Anyway*, Arrow Books, 1991

Kennerley, Helen, *Overcoming Anxiety*, Robinson, 1998

Lindenfield, Gael, *Assert Yourself, Super Confidence, Self-Motivation, Self-Esteem, Emotional Confidence, The Positive Woman*, Thorsons

McGraw, Philip, *Life Strategies*, Vermilion, 1998

McKay, Matthew and Patrick Fanning, *Self-Esteem*, New Harbinger, 2000

Northrup, Christiane, *Women's Bodies, Women's Wisdom*, Bantam, 1995

Patent, Arnold, *You Can Have It All*, Newleaf, 1995

Peck, M. Scott, *The Road Less Travelled*, Touchstone, 1978

Redfield, *Celestine Prophesy*, Warner, 1993

Root, Dr Brian, *The Confidence To Be Yourself*, Piatkus, 1998

Smith, Manuel J., *When I Say No, I Feel Guilty*, Bantam, 1975

Taylor, Ros, *Confidence in Just Seven Days*, Vermilion, 2000

Peale, Norman Vincent, *The Power of Positive Thinking and You Can If You Think You Can*, Vermilion

Webber, Christine, *Get the Happiness Habit*, Hodder & Stoughton, 2000

USEFUL ADDRESSES

The best sources of information are:

1. Your GP or doctor, who will have details of local services available.
2. Yellow pages – look under counselling and advice, psychotherapy, analysis.
3. Citizen's Advice Bureau.
4. Councils of Community Service.
5. Local newspapers and churches often provide helpful telephone numbers.

Certain organisations, phone helplines, websites and support groups can offer advice about improving self-esteem and problems that can affect self-esteem. Here are some of the most well known and respected. Where no phone number is supplied, send a SAE for information.

IRELAND

AA Dublin Service Office
109 South Circular Road
Leonards Corner
Dublin 8
Tel: 01 4538998

Al-Anon Information Centre
5-6 Capel Street
Dublin 1
Tel: 01 8732699

The Mental Health Association of Ireland
Mensana House
6 Adelaide Street
Dun Laoghaire
Co. Dublin
Tel: 01 2841166

Aware – Helping to Defeat Depression
147 Phibsborough Road
Dublin 7
Tel: 01 8308449

Samaritans
112 Marlborough Street
Dublin 1
Tel: 01 8727700
Helpline: 1850 609090

Dublin County Stress Clinic
St John of God Hospital
Stillorgan
Co. Dublin
Tel: 01 2881781

Bereavement Counselling Service
Dublin Street
Baldoyle
Co. Dublin
Tel: 01 8391766

Irish Association for Counselling
and Therapy
8 Cumberland Street
Dun Laoghaire
Co. Dublin
Tel: 01 2300061

Irish Association of Psychotherapy
17 Dame Court
Dublin 2
Tel: 01 6794055

Victim Support
29 Dame Street
Dublin 2
Tel: 01 6798673

Yoga Fellowship of Northern
Ireland
16 Kinghill Road
Rathfriland
Co. Down BT34 5RB
Tel: 018206 31138

Yoga
An Sanctoir
Ballydehob
Co. Cork
Tel: 021 284336

Age Concern Northern Ireland
3 Lower Crescent
Belfast B7 1NR
Tel: 028 90233323

UNITED KINGDOM
Addiction
Alcoholics Anonymous
PO Box 1
Stonebow House
Stonebow
York YO1 2NJ
Tel: 01904 644026
(for local Helpline numbers)

Al-Anon Family Groups
61 Great Dover Street
London SE1 4YF
Tel: 0207 4030888

Narcotics Anonymous
UK Service Office
PO Box 1980
London N19 3LS
Tel: 0207 7300009

National Drugs Helpline:
0800 776600

Institute of Drug Dependency
Waterbridge House
32–36 London Street
London EC1 OEE
Tel: 0207 9281211

Assertiveness training

The Industrial Society runs courses in assertiveness.
Tel: 0870 4001000

Debt

Citizens Advice Bureau
For local address, see your phone book under C or Yellow Pages under Counselling and Advice.

National Debtline
Birmingham Settlement
318 Summer Lane
Birmingham B18 3RL
Tel: 0121 3598501

Family Welfare Association
501–505 Kingsland Road
London E8 4AU
Tel: 0207 2546251

Depression

Depression Alliance
35 Westminster Bridge Road
London SE1 7JB
Tel: 0207 2073293
www.depressionalliance.org

MIND (National Association for Mental Health)
Granta House
15–19 Broadway
London E15 4BQ
Tel: 0208 5192122

MIND information line:
0345 660163; 08457 660163 outside greater London;
0208 5221728 London
www.mind.org.uk

Seasonal Affective Disorder Association
PO Box 989
London SW7 2PZ
Tel: 01903 814942

Eating Disorders Association
First Floor
Wensum House
103 Prince of Wales Road
Norwich
Norfolk NR1 1DW
Tel: 01603 621414

Lesbian and Gay Issues
London Lesbian and Gay
Switchboard
PO Box 7324
London N1 9QS
Tel: 0207 8377324
www.llgs.org.uk/info.htm

Homelessness
Shelter
Tel: 0207 2530202
London Helpline: 0800 446441
Local Shelter Housing Advice line
listed in the Yellow Pages under
Information Services.

Health
NHS Direct
Tel: 0845 46 47

Health Education Authority
Trevelyan House
30 Peter Street
London SW1P 2HW
Tel: 0207 2225300

General advice on healthy living,
diet and exercise.

British Heart Foundation
14 Fitzhardinge Street
London W1H 4DH
Tel: 0207 9350185

AIDS Helpline
Tel: 0800 56712

Cancer Link
Tel: 0800 132905

British Pregnancy Advisory service
Tel: 01564 793225

Relationship and Family Problems
Counciliation Services
Family Mediation Scotland:
Tel: 0131 2201610
Family Mediation Association:
Tel: 0207 8819400
National Family Mediation:
Tel: 0207 3835993

CRUSE Bereavement Care
Cruse House
126 Sheen Road
Richmond
Surrey TW9 1UR
Tel: 0208 9404818

Age Concern
Astral House
1268 London Road
London SW16 4ER
Tel: 0800 731 4931

Anti-bullying Campaign
185 Tower Bridge Road
London SE1 2UF
Tel: 0207 3781446

Family Crisis Line
c/o Ashwood House
Ashwood Road
Woking
Surrey GU22 7JW
Tel: 01483 722533

Exploring Parenthood
4 Ivory Place
20a Treadgold Street
London W11 4BP
Tel: 0207 2216681

Institute of Family Therapy
24-32 Stephenson Way
London NW1 2HX
Tel: 0207 3919150

Parentline
Endway House
The Endway
Hadleigh
Essex SS7 2AN
Tel: 01702 559900

Relate (National Marriage
Guidance Council)
Herbert Gray College
Little Church Street
Rugby
Warickshire CV21 3AP
Tel: 01788 573241
www.relate.org.uk

British Association for Sexual and
Relationship Therapy
PO Box 13686
London SW20 9ZH

Institute of Psychosexual Medicine
11 Chandos Street
Cavendish Square
London W1M 9DE
Tel: 0207 5800631

Single Concern Group Support Group
PO Box 4
High Street
Goring-on-Thames
Oxon RG8 9DN
Tel: 01491 873195
For lonely and socially isolated
men and women.

Families Need Fathers
134 Curtain Road
London EC2A 3AR
Tel: 0207 6135060
Support for fathers living apart
from their children.

More-to-Life
114 Lichfield Street
Walsall WS1 ISZ
Tel: 070 500 37905
www.moretolife.co.uk
Support group for people without children.

Telephone Helplines

The Samaritans
General Office
10 The Grove
Slough SL1 1QP
Tel: 01753 532713
24-hour Helpline: 08457 909090
or 0345 909090

Careline
Cardinal Heenan Centre
326-8 High Road
Ilford
Essex 1G1 1QP
Tel: 0208 514 5444; 0208 514 1177
Counselling on all issues.

Youth Access
1a Taylor's Yard
67 Alderbrook Road
London SW12 8AD
Tel: 0208 7729900
Counselling for young people and children.

Therapy/Counselling

Traumatic Stress Clinic
73 Charlotte Street
London W1P 1LB
Tel: 0207 4369000

The British Psychological
Association
St Andrew's House
48 Princess Road East
Leicester LE1 7DR
Tel: 0116 2549568
www.bps.org.uk

British Association of Behavioural
and Cognitive Psychotherapists
(BABCP)
PO Box 9
Accrington BB5 2GD

The British Association of
Psychotherapists
37 Mapesbury Road
London NW2 4HJ
Tel: 0208 8305173
www.bcp.org.uk

UK Council for Psychotherapy
Regent's College
Inner Circle
Regent's Park
London NW1 4NS
Tel: 0207 4363002

The British Association for
Counselling
1 Regent's Place
Rugby
Warwickshire CV21 2BJ
Tel: 01788 550899

Victim support
Talk to your GP if you are an adult
victim of childhood abuse.

Childline
Freepost 1111
London N1 0BR
Tel: 0800 1111

Rape Crisis Centre
PO Box 69
London WC1X 9NJ
Tel: 0207 8371600

Survivors
PO Box 2470
London SW 9 9ZP
Tel: 0207 8333737
Support for men who have been
raped.

Victim Support
Tel: 0845 3030900

Women's Aid
Tel: 0345 023468
For women in violent relationships.

Alternative Therapies
Institute for Complementary
Medicine
PO Box 194
London SE16 IQZ
Tel: 0207 2375165

Council for Complementary and
Alternative Medicine
179 Gloucester Place
London NW1 6DX
Tel: 0208 7350632

British Wheel of Yoga
1 Hamilton Place
Boston Road
Sleaford
Lincolnshire NG34 7ES
Tel: 01529 306851

US
24-hour line: 1 888 8 ANXIETY
1 888 8 269438

American Association for Counseling
5999 Stevenson Avenue
Alexandria
VA 22304
Tel: 703 823 9840

International Association of
Counselors and Therapists
8313 West Hillsborough Avenue

Suite 480
Tampa
Florida 33615
Tel: 813 877 5592

Freedom from Fear
308 Seaview Avenue
Staten Island
NY 10305
Tel: 718 351 1717

Depression Awareness, Recognition
and Treatment (DART)
National Institute of Mental Health
5600 Fishers Lane
Rockville
MD 20857
Tel: 800 421 4211

National Foundation for
Depressive Illness (NAFDI)
PO Box 2257
New York
NY 10116
Tel: 800 248 4344

National Mental Health
Consumer's Self-Help Information
Clearinghouse
211 Chestnut Street, Suite 1000
Philadelphia
PA 19107
Tel: 215 751 1810
Tel: 800 553 4539

Depression and Related Affective
Disorders Association (DRADA)
Meyer 3-181
600 North Wolfe Street
Baltimore
MD 21287-7381
Tel: 410 955 4647

American Psychological
Association
750 1st Street, NE
Washington
DC 20002
Tel: 202 336 5500

American Psychiatric Association
1400 K Street NW
Washington
DC 20005
Tel: 202 682 6066

Association for Advancement of
Behavior Therapy
305 Seventh Avenue
New York
NY 10001
Tel: 212 647 1890

Administration on Aging
330 Independence Avenue SW
Washington DC 20201
Tel: 202 619 0724

American Anorexia/Bulimia
Association
293 Central Park West
Suite 1R
New York
NY 10024
Tel: 212 501 8351

AIDS Hotline
Tel: 800 342 AIDS

American Association of
Naturopathic Physicians
PO Box 20386
Seattle
WA 98102
Tel: 206 323 7610

American Yoga Association
513 South Orange Avenue
Sarasta
FL 34236
AmYogaAssn@aol.com

Anxiety Disorders Association of
America
6000 Executive Boulevard
Suite 513
Rockville
MD 20852
Tel: 301 231 9350

Al-Anon Family Group
Headquarters
Tel: 212 302 7240

Alcoholics Anonymous World
Services
Tel: 212 870 3400

National Association on
Alcoholism and Drug Dependence
12 West 21 Street
New York
NY 10010
Tel: 800 NCA-CALL

THE INEVITABLE WISE PROVERB ... OR TWO

All self-help books have proverbs. I couldn't resist finishing with just one or two. If they don't make sense, you haven't read the book.

> We are what we think.
> All that we are arises from our thoughts.
> With our thoughts we make the world.
> The Dhammapada: *The Sayings of the Buddha*

> People with high self-esteem
> Have it because
> They have overcome their failures.
> They have been put to the test of life
> Overcome the problems and grown.
> *David Jansen*

```
250  yd
300.  yd
3.00  Sl.
750  Ol
1 50  -
150  krd
150  RR
─────────
2050
```